Fascinating String Figures

International String Figure Association

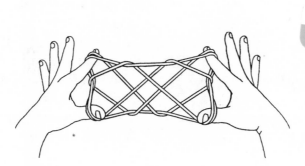

DOVER PUBLICATIONS, INC.
Mineola, New York

Contents

Published in Canada by General Publishing Company, Ltd., 30 Lesmill Road, Don Mills, Toronto, Ontario.
Published in the United Kingdom by Constable and Company, Ltd., 3 The Lanchesters, 162–164 Fulham Palace Road, London W6 9ER.

Illustrations and text by Mark A. Sherman and Joseph D'Antoni
Design and layout by Mark A. Sherman

Bibliographical Note

Fascinating String Figures, first published by Dover Publications, Inc., in 1999, is an original compilation of material first published in issues of *String Figure Magazine,* (ISFA Press, Pasadena, California), in 1996 and 1997.

The International String Figure Association was founded in 1978. Members submitting annual dues receive the quarterly *String Figure Magazine* (ISSN 1087-1527), the annual *Bulletin of the International String Figure Association* (ISSN 1076-7886), and the semi-annual *ISFA News.*

For membership information, write to ISFA, P.O. Box 5134, Pasadena, California, 91117, USA, or visit the ISFA on the World Wide Web (www.isfa.org/~webweavers/isfa.htm).

Library of Congress Cataloging-in-Publication Data

Fascinating string figures / International String Figure Association.
  p.   cm.
  "Compilation of material first published in issues of String figure magazine (ISFA Press, Pasadena, California) in 1996 and 1997"—T.p. verso.
  Includes index.
  ISBN 0-486-40400-5 (pbk.)
  1. String figures. I. International String Figure Association. II. String figure magazine.
GV1218.S8F37   1999
793.9'6—dc21   98-43435
                                                       CIP

Manufactured in the United States of America
Dover Publications, Inc., 31 East 2nd Street, Mineola, N.Y. 11501

Getting Started - fingers, loops, strings, and commands

1 String

Almost any type of string can be used to make string figures — nylon, polyester, or cotton to name a few. Most of the string figures in this issue were made with cotton utility cord measuring 1/8" (4 mm) in thickness. To make a 2-foot loop, join the ends of a 4-foot segment; for a 3-foot loop use a 6-foot segment, and so forth...

Making an endless loop from nylon or polyester string is easy. Simply flame the ends until they melt, then touch them together. The bond forms instantly. To make a loop from cotton string, smear a little molten nylon on the ends, reflame briefly, then touch them together. Too much trouble? — remember, you can always join the ends with a knot!

2 Fingers

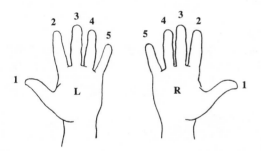

The fingers of each hand are numbered 1 through 5, starting with the thumb.
L and R stand for "Left" and "Right."

Examples
- 3 means "middle finger of each hand."
- L1 means "left thumb"
- R4 means "right ring finger"

3 Loop names and commands

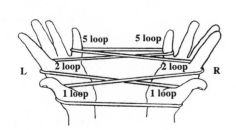

Loops are named after the fingers they surround. In this illustration of "Opening A" there is a *1 loop*, a *2 loop*, and a *5 loop* on each hand.

When making string figures, loops are often *released*, *transferred*, *rotated*, *exchanged*, *shared*, or *navahoed*.

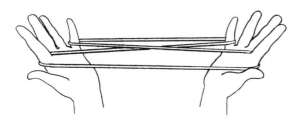

Release 1 loop means..."Let the loop on finger 1 of each hand slip off, then separate the hands to absorb the slack."

To transfer a loop from one finger to another, we use the command *remove*.

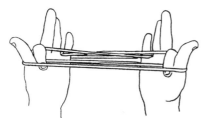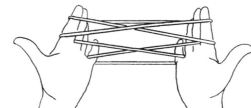

2, from below, removes 1 loop means..."Finger 2, from below, enters the loop on finger 1, then finger 1 releases its loop."

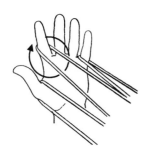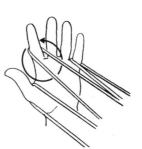

A loop can also be removed *from above*, in which case the loop is inverted.

Since hands and fingers are not always held in an upright position when making string figures, we define *above* to mean "from the fingertip side" and *below* to mean "from the knuckle side." Experts often use the terms *distal* and *proximal* to avoid confusion.

To twist a loop, we use the command *rotate*. A loop can be rotated *away from you* (in the direction of finger 5) or *towards you* (in the direction of finger 1).

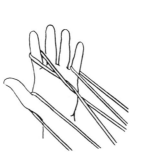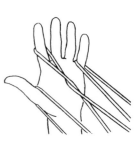

Rotate L2 loop a full turn away from you.   *Rotate L2 loop a full turn towards you.*

A loop can also be rotated a *half turn* in either direction, but this requires lifting the loop off the finger with the opposite hand, rotating it, and replacing it (not shown).

To pass a loop on one hand through a loop on the other, we use the command *exchange*.

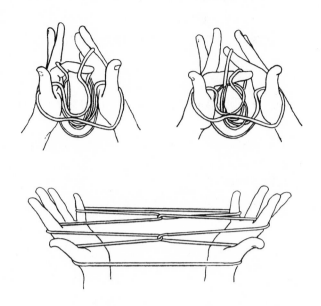

Exchange 2 loops, inserting 2 from above, passing R loop through L loop means...

"Bring fingertips together and insert left finger 2, from above (i.e., from the fingertip side), into the loop on right finger 2...then withdraw right finger 2 and insert it, from above, into the lower loop on left finger 2 (i.e., the loop nearest the knuckle) and lift the lower loop off the left finger, over the upper loop (i.e., the loop nearest the fingertip)...then separate the hands to complete the exchange."

To create two loops from one, we use the command *share*.

 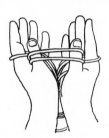 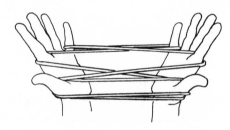

Share the 1 loops, inserting R1 first means...

"Bring the hands together and insert right finger 1, from below, into the loop on left finger 1...then withdraw left finger 1 and insert it, from below, into both loops on right finger 1...and separate the hands.

To pass one loop through a second loop on the same finger, we use the command *navaho*.

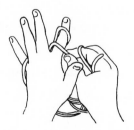 

Navaho 2 loops means...

"With the help of the opposite hand (or your mouth) lift the lower loop on finger 2 over the upper loop on finger 2 and release it.

Kathleen Haddon coined the term in 1912 after noticing that the technique is common among the Navaho people of the American Southwest.

4 String names and commands

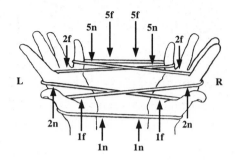

Each loop has a near string (n) and a far string (f).

Examples
- *2n* means "the near string of the loop on each finger 2."
- *L2f* means "the far string of the loop on the left finger 2."

When making a string figure, strings are either *picked up*, *hooked up*, or *hooked down*...

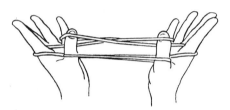

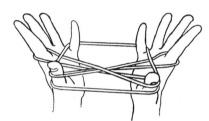

1, over 2 loop, picks up 5n means..."Pass finger 1 of each hand away from you, over the loop on finger 2, then with the nail side of finger 1 catch the near string of the loop on finger 5 and return finger 1 to its original position."

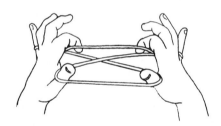

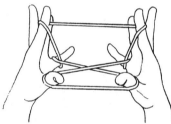

2, over 5n, hooks up 5f means..."Pass finger 2 of each hand away from you, over the near string of the loop on finger 5, then, with the fingerprint side of finger 2, catch the far string of the loop on finger 5 and return finger 2 to its original position, in this case by rotating it half a turn towards you."

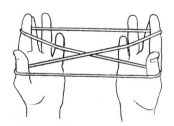

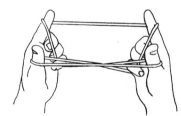

5, under 2f, hooks down 2n, closing it to the palm means... "With the fingerprint side of finger 5 of each hand, press down on the near string of the loop surrounding finger 2 of each hand until the fingertip of finger 5 touches the palm."

Special Note: On the pages that follow, each drawing shows what you should see on your hands **after** completing the instructions associated with the illustration. Instructions in *italics* prepare you for the next move.

Night

-collected by Lyle A. Dickey from the people of the Hawaiian Islands

Recommended Loop Size: 3 feet

The native name for this figure is *Po*, meaning "night" or "darkness." Long ago, nearly every Hawaiian knew how to make it. In Polynesian mythology *Po* represents chaos: "In the beginning there was nothing but *Po*, a void without light, heat, sound, form, or motion..."

1

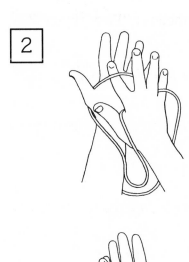

Place loop on 1 and 5.

Locate the left palmar string (Lp), and the right palmar string (Rp).

2

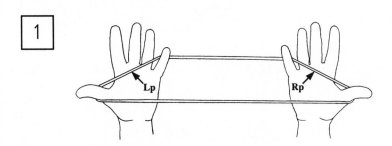

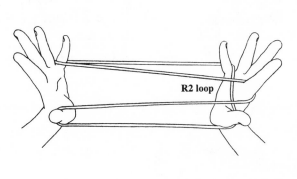

R2 picks up Lp...extend.

Locate the R2 loop.

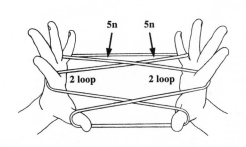

L2, through R2 loop from above, picks up Rp...extend. You have "Opening A."

Locate the 2 loop and the 5n string.

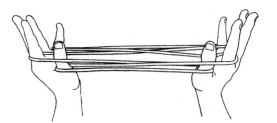

Insert finger 1, from below, into the 2 loop...

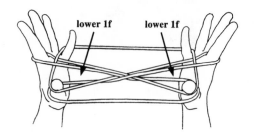

...then pick up 5n and return through the 2 loop.

Locate the lower 1f string.

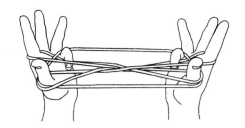

Insert finger 5, from above, into the 2 loop...

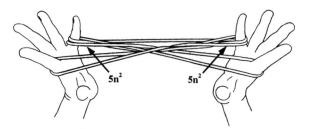

...then pick up lower 1f and return through the 2 loop.

Locate the double 1 loop (1 loop^2).

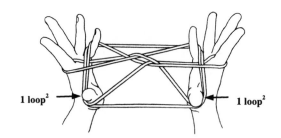

Release 1 loop^2 and extend.

Locate the double 5n string (5n^2).

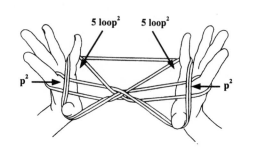

1, over 2 loop, picks up 5n^2.

Locate the double palmar string (p^2) and the double 5 loop (5 loop^2).

6

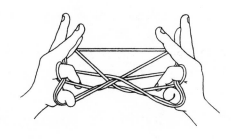

Insert 2, from above into its own loop (over p^2)...

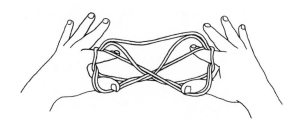

...Release 5 loop^2...

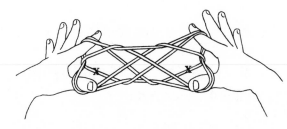

...then extend the figure by rotating finger 2 away and up. You have "Night." The seven diamonds represent stars.

Locate the string labeled "X".

In the string figure literature string "X" is often described as an "oblique string which crosses the 1 loop" or the "string which runs from the palmar string to the lower transverse string."

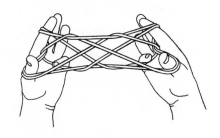

To make the stars disappear, use 5 to hook down string "X"...

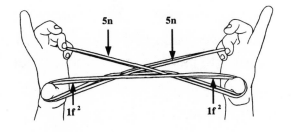

...then release the double 2 loop and extend. This represents "Dawn".

Locate the 5n string and the double 1f string ($1f^2$).

Throughout the day the stars remain hidden from view. But as dusk approaches they begin to reappear. To make the stars reappear, do the following:

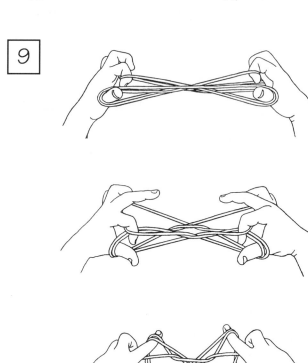

2 enters the 5 loop from above and hooks 5n toward you...

...then 2 enters the double 1 loop...

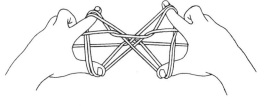

...and hooks up 1f ^{2} (5n slips off finger 2 as you rotate it away and up)...

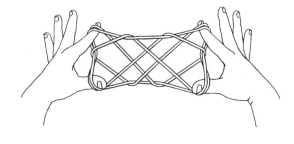

...Release the 5 loop and extend sharply. You have "Night" once again.

You can repeat Steps 8 and 9 as often as you like. Each repetition represents the perpetual cycle of day and night.

This figure is known throughout the Pacific. It has also been recorded in Japan, Africa, and South America. The method for making it differs from place to place, and in some locations, like Hawaii, two methods are known!

Twinkling Star

-collected by Lyle A. Dickey from the people of the Hawaiian Islands

Recommended Loop Size: 3 feet

This figure, also known throughout the Hawaiian Islands, is a continuation of "Night."

Start with "Night."

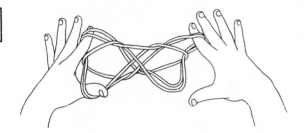

R1 gently releases its double loop...

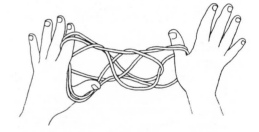

...then R1, from below, removes the double R2 loop...

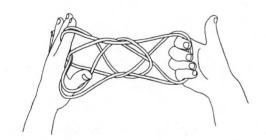

...and R2345, from above, remove the double R1 loop. Close R2345 to the palm to secure the double string.

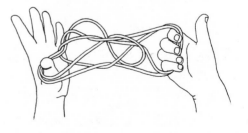

Next, L2 gently releases its double loop...

9

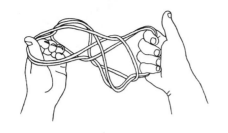

...and L2345, from below, remove the double L1 loop...

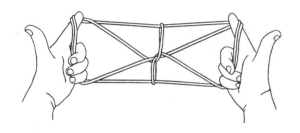

Close L2345 to the palm to secure the double string...

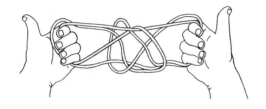

...then straighten finger 2 to extend the figure. You have the Hawaiian "Star".

12

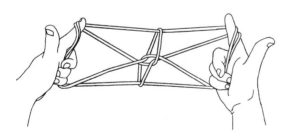

To make the star "twinkle", shift finger 2 of each hand from side to side, first to the right...

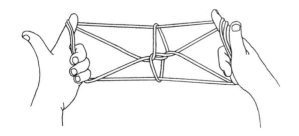

...then to the left.

The near strings of the central design will slide past the far strings, much like a pair of scissors, and the central diamond will open and close to imitate "twinkling".

Seven Diamonds

-collected by Will Wirt from children of Brillo Nuevo, northeastern Peru

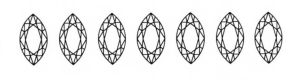

Recommended Loop Size: 4 feet

This figure introduces a novel technique for adding extra diamonds to a simple diamond figure. The technique involves repeating the "navaho" move more than once. Each extra navaho adds a pair of diamonds to the figure. Here, two extra navahos (a triple navaho) are used to add four diamonds to a three-diamond pattern, giving seven diamonds. For added fun, also try a single navaho (three diamonds), a double navaho (five diamonds), or a quadruple navaho (nine diamonds). A thin string is recommended.

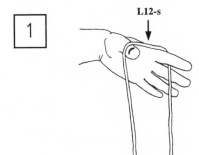

| 1 |

To begin, hang a loop on L1 and L2.

Locate the short segment of string that joins L1 and L2 (L12-s).

| 2 |

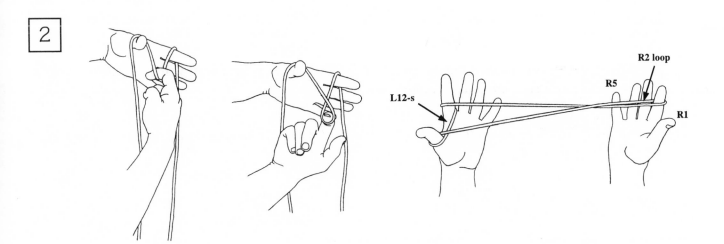

With R2 hook down L12-s...then rotate R2 toward you to create a half twist in the loop...Reposition the hands and extend.

Again locate L12-s (newly created during step 2), fingers R1 and R5, and the R2 loop.

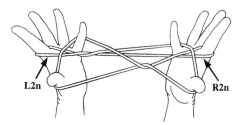

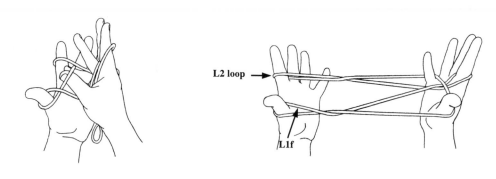

Bring R1 and R5 together above the R2 loop, then use them to pick up L12-s ...Extend. *Locate the L1f string and the L2 loop.*

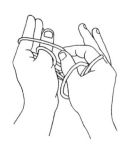

L5, over the L2 loop, picks up L1f.

Locate the L2n string and the R2n string (segments close to finger 2).

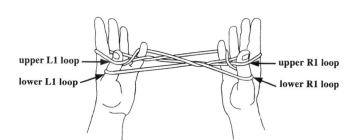

With the help of the R hand, draw out L2n and place it on the tip of L1. Repeat on the opposite hand (not shown)...and extend.

On each hand locate the upper and lower 1 loops. Note that the upper 1 loop also encircles finger 2.

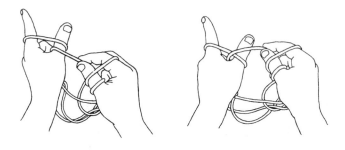

Now perform a triple Navaho move:

First, with the help of the R hand, lift the lower L1 loop over the upper L1 loop, *but do not release it from L1* (simply move it to the upper position)...

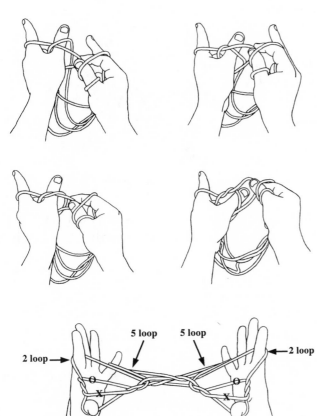

...Second, grasp the new lower L1 loop and lift it over the new upper L1 loop, *but again, do not release it from L1* (simply move it to the upper position)...

...Third, grasp the new lower L1 loop and again lift it over the new upper L1 loop, *but this time release it from L1...*

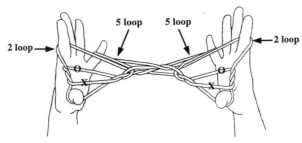

...Likewise, perform the triple navaho move on R1 and extend.

Locate the 2 loop, the 5 loop, and the string segments labeled "X" and "O".

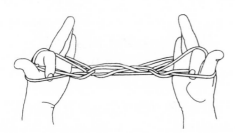

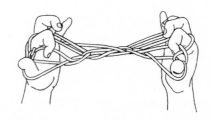

7

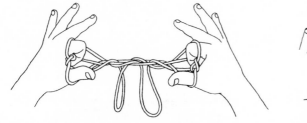

With 2 hook string "X" away from you,...carry it over string "O" and insert the tip of 2, from above, into the 2 loop.

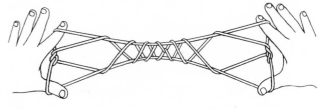

Release the 5 loop,...draw string "X" through the 2 loop (which slips off), and rotate finger 2 away from you and up to extend the figure. You have "Seven Diamonds."

Polar Bear

-collected by Diamond Jenness from the Inuit of Northern Alaska

Recommended Loop Size: 3 feet

This classic Inuit (Eskimo) figure is a variation of *Swan,* which appears on page 44. In fact Steps 1 through 8, in which a two-diamond "loom" is created, are identical in both figures.

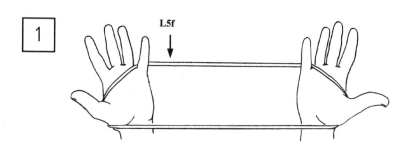

Place loop on 1 and 5.

Locate the left segment of the 5f string (L5f).

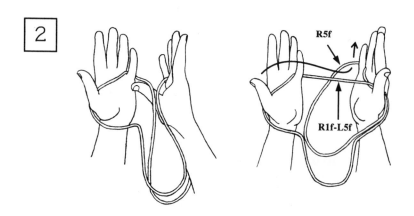

R1, *over* L5f, picks up L5f...
...Extend partially.

Locate the R1f-L5f string and the R5f string.

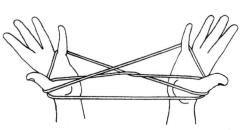

L1, over R1f-L5f (but under R5f), picks up R5f. Extend.

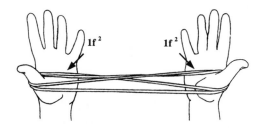

Release 5 loop. *Locate the double 1f string.*

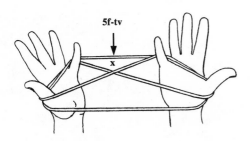

5 picks up 1f[2].

Locate the 5f string which is transverse* (5f-tv).

*A transverse string is a string that runs straight across the figure between two like fingers, in this case R5 and L5.

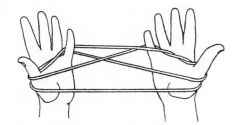

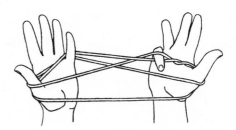

Allow 5f-tv to slip off R5...

...then close R5 to the palm over it...

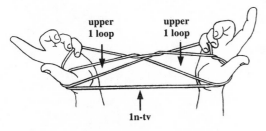

Repeat on L5 and extend.

Note: this move is tricky! In slipping 5f-tv, you need to pass 5 of each hand down through the triangle marked "x" in the Step 5 illustration, then up behind 5f-tv before closing it to the palm.

Locate the 1n-tv string and the upper 1 loop.

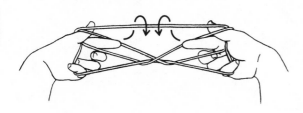

Insert 2, from above, into the upper 1 loop (shown here is the view from below) then curl 2 around 1n-tv...

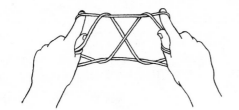

...and return with it through the upper 1 loop by rotating 2 away and up.

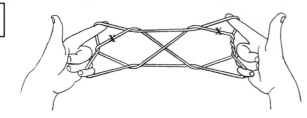

Release 1 loops and extend. You now have a "two-diamond" pattern.

Before proceeding, carefully examine all the string crossings to make sure they match the picture. If they don't, you won't get a Polar Bear at the end! Once you're convinced everything is O.K., locate the string segment labeled "X".

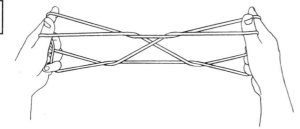

With 1 pick up the string segment labeled "X".

You are now ready for a right-handed katilluik maneuver. It's right-handed because R1 is inserted first.

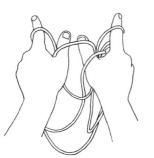 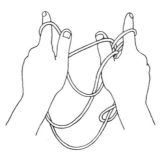 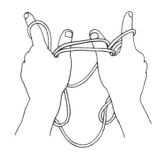

Share the 1 loops, inserting R1 first (see page 3 for a full explanation)...

...and extend.

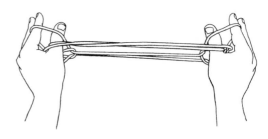

Insert 1, from below, into the 2 loop...

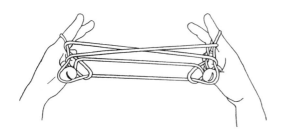

...then navaho the loops on 1 (lower double loop over upper single loop) to complete the katilluik maneuver. See page 3 for a full description of the navaho move.

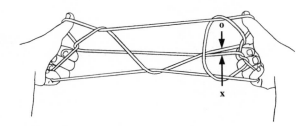

Release the 2 loop and extend, 1 pointing upward.

Locate the string segments labeled "x" and "o".

Inuits frequently employ the manipulations shown below (Steps 12 and 13) in weaving animal figures. For example, the same sequence is used in weaving "A Dog with Large Ears" (see page 59) and "Swan" (see page 44).

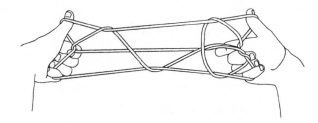

With R2 hook up strings "x" and "o"...

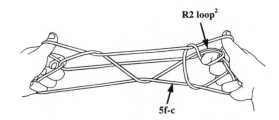

...then insert R2, from "above" (i.e., from the fingertip side) into the R1 loop.

Locate the double R2 loop (R2 loop^2) and the central segment of the 5f string (5f-c).

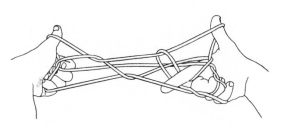

With R2 hook up 5f-c...

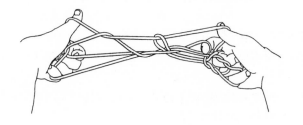

...and draw it through the R2 loop^2, which slips off. Note that the tip of R2 remains inserted, from above, into the R1 loop...

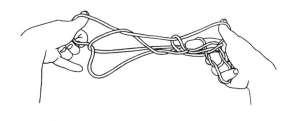

...Gently release the L5 loop...

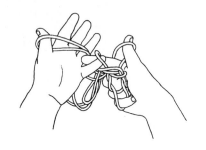

...then insert L5, from "above" (i.e., from the fingertip side), into the R2 loop...

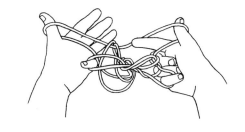

...and remove the loop from R2, closing L5 to the left palm...

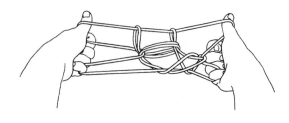

...Extend, 1 pointing upward.

You now have an upside-down Polar Bear!

14

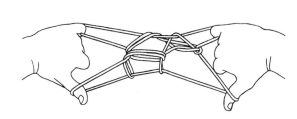

To invert the figure, rotate each hand 180° so that the palms face away from you (i.e., point finger 1 toward you, then down).

Stand back and admire the magnificent Polar Bear!

"Polar Bear" is also known to the Inuit of Canada (Mackenzie Delta, Coronation Gulf, and Pelly Bay). You'll even find it in Greenland along the southwest coast, and at Thule.

Ever wonder what sound a polar bear makes? At Pelly Bay, the Inuit chant "heuuuu, heuuuu" as they display this figure!

Turtle

-A Modern String Figure from Japan

Recommended Loop Size: 2 feet

This string figure has appeared in many wonderfully illustrated Ayatori books published in Japan. The oldest reference to this figure may be in a 1980 book written by Hiroshi Noguchi.

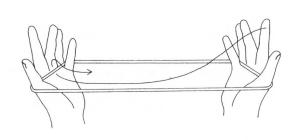

Place loop on 1 and 5 of each hand.

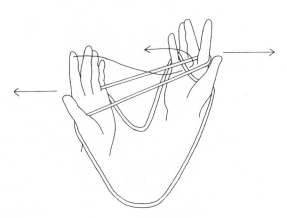

R2 picks up Lp...extend slightly.

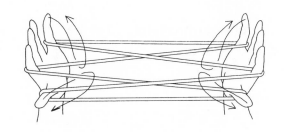

L2, through R2 loop from above, picks up Rp...extend.

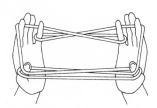

Insert 1 and 5, from below, into the 2 loop.

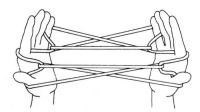

 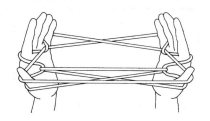

Navaho 1 loops and 5 loops.

A transverse string surrounds the 2f-5n segment of each hand. 1 goes over intermediate strings and picks up the transverse string.

 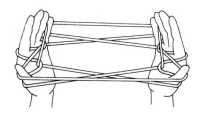

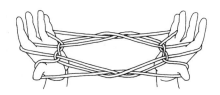

A transverse string surrounds the 1f-2n segment of each hand. 5 goes over intermediate strings and picks up the transverse string.

Navaho 1 loops and 5 loops.

 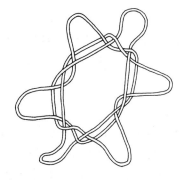

With fingers pointed up, lay the figure onto a surface, and arrange.

A Baby Being Born

-collected by Daniel Sutherland Davidson from the Wardaman Aborigines of North Australia.

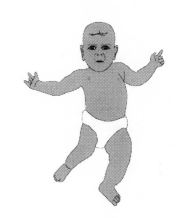

Recommended Loop Size: 3 feet

This sliding figure simulates a baby dropping from a mother's womb.

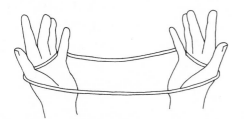

Place the loop on 1 and 5 of each hand.

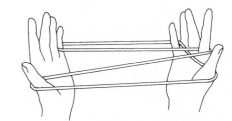

R2 picks up Lp...extend.

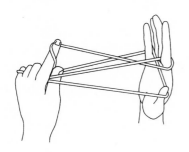

L1 picks up L5n.

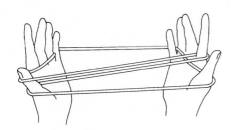

Bend L2 over Lp and pick up L1f, and simultaneously trap this string between upright 1 and 2.

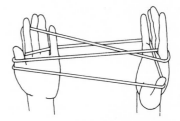

Turn left hand so that palm faces away. Notice that during the rotation the L2 string winds about L2, and L345 bend down over L5f. This and the previous movement is known as the *Caroline Extension*.

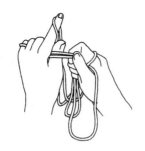

Bring hands together, and with R1 and R2 grasp the two strings originating from the base of 1. Note that one of these strings leads to L2, and the other one leads to L5.

Left hand releases all strings. Carefully arrange the strings held by R1 and R2 so that the former L2 string becomes the far string and the former L5 string becomes the near string. Then press L1 and L5 together...

...and pass these two fingers between the arranged strings so that L5 picks up the far string and L1 picks up the near string.

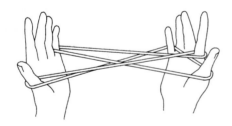

R1 and R2 release their strings and extend.

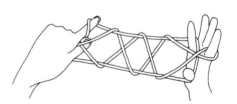

Repeat Steps 3 through 8 two more times, then repeat Steps 3 through 5.

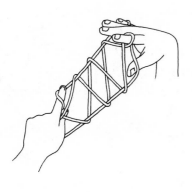

Reorient the hands so that right is above left.

The three diamonds represent the baby.

 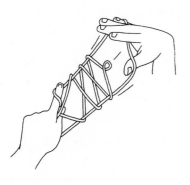

Release R2 loop...

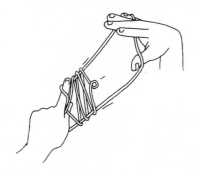

...and the baby drops from the mother's womb.

R2 can repeatedly pick up and release the sliding string to simulate multiple births.

Cobweb

-collected by Johannes Carl Andersen from a Maori youth (Whanganui tribe), New Zealand

Recommended Loop Size: 6 feet. Also needed is a 7-foot length of string.

At least two players are required for this figure. Andersen recommends three: two to form the figure and one to thread a string through the design.

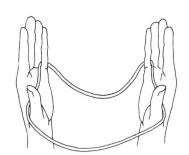

Place the loop on 1 and 5 of each hand.

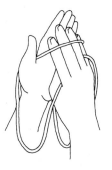 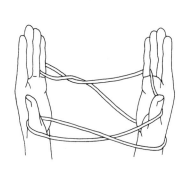

The five fingers of the right hand pick up Lp...extend.

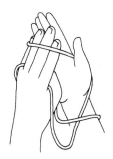 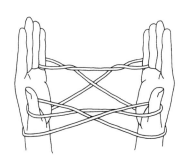

The five fingers of the left hand pick up Rp...extend.

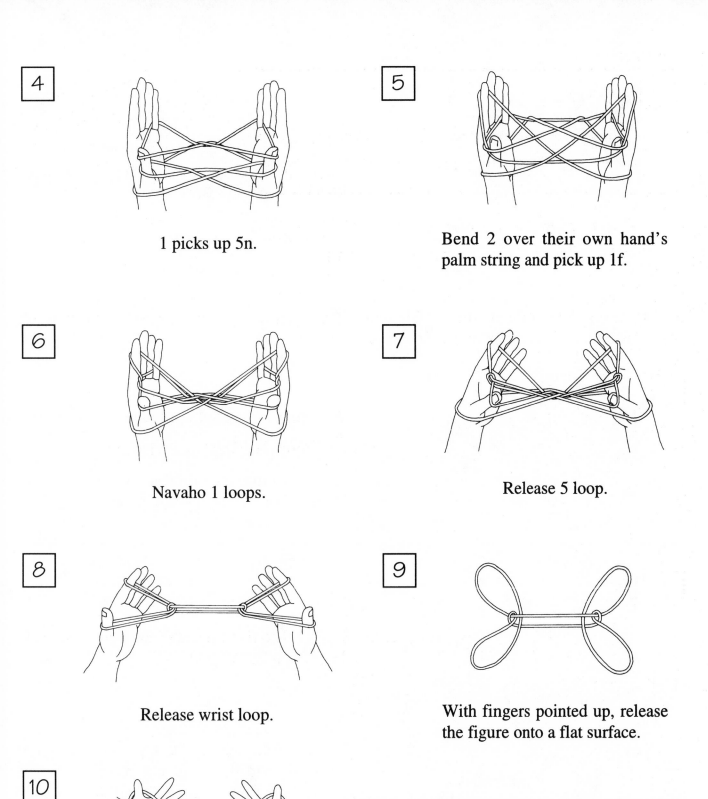

4

1 picks up 5n.

5

Bend 2 over their own hand's palm string and pick up 1f.

6

Navaho 1 loops.

7

Release 5 loop.

8

Release wrist loop.

9

With fingers pointed up, release the figure onto a flat surface.

10

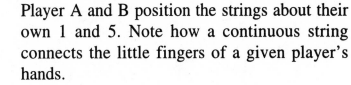

Player A and B position the strings about their own 1 and 5. Note how a continuous string connects the little fingers of a given player's hands.

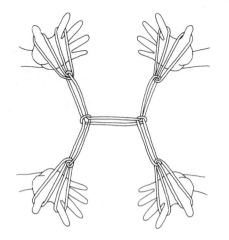

Both players perform the movements illustrated in Steps 2 through 8.

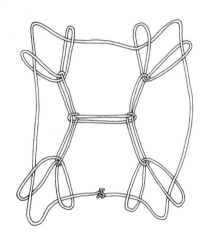

With fingers pointed up, both players release the figure onto a flat surface.

Thread another length of string through each loop, and tie the free ends together.

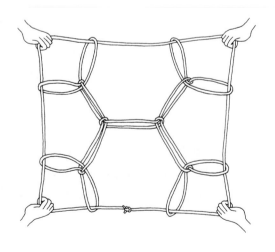

To extend the cobweb, each player takes hold of the threaded string and forms a rough square. The figure can be displayed vertically or horizontally — it's your choice!

Catching a Cockroach

-collected by Peter H. Buck from the
people of Samoa, South Pacific

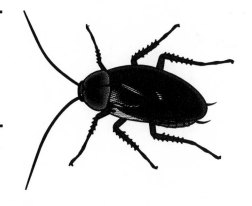

Recommended Loop Size: 2 feet

This simple figure is a "catch" requiring the finger of a second player. How many cockroaches can you catch?

<table>
<tr><td>

1

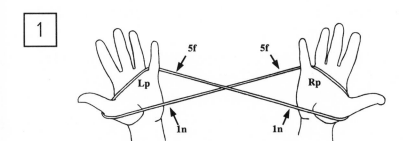

</td><td>

Place loop on 1 and 5 so that 1n and 5f cross.

Locate the L palmar string (Lp), and the R palmar string (Rp).

</td></tr>
<tr><td>

2

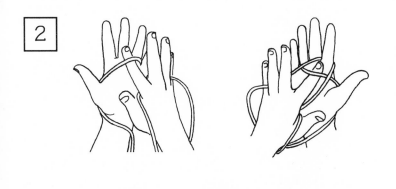

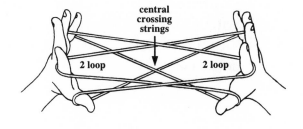

</td><td>

R2 picks up Lp...

...L2, through R2 loop from above, picks up Rp...

...Extend.

Locate the 2 loop and the central crossing strings (1n and 5f).

</td></tr>
</table>

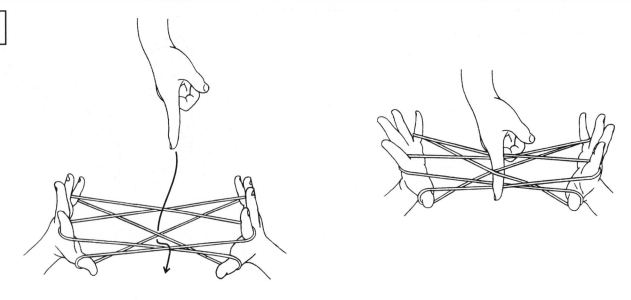

Next, ask a friend to pass her R2 finger down through your 2 loop...then toward you under the central crossing strings...then up through your 2 loop.

Your friend's finger represents the cockroach.

4

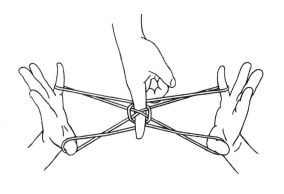

Without warning, release the 2 loop on each hand and extend sharply. You just caught a cockroach!

5

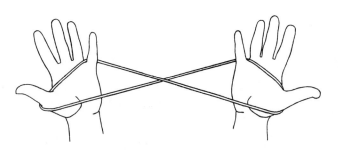

To repeat the trick, ask your friend to withdraw her finger, then extend. You are now ready to catch another cockroach!

28

A Hammock

-collected by James Hornell from a
Muhammadan boy of Zanzibar
Island, Tanzania

Recommended Loop Size: 3 feet

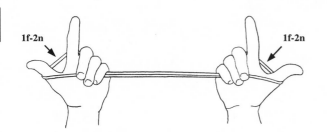

1   Place loop on 1 and 2.

Locate the 1n string and the 2f string, both being transverse strings.

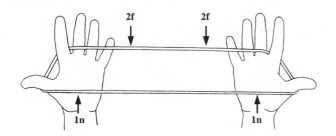

2   3, 4, and 5 hook down 2f and 1n, closing them to the palm.

Locate the short string that joins finger 1 and 2 (the 1f-2n string).

3

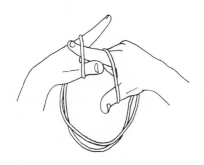

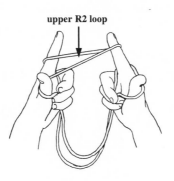

R2 picks up the short 1f-2n string of the L hand...

...extend partially to create an upper R2 loop...

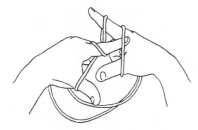

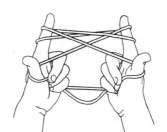

L2, over upper R2 loop, picks up the short 1f-2n string of the R hand...

...extend partially...

29

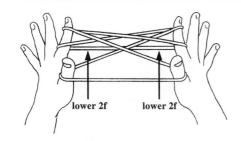

Release 3, 4, and 5, and extend fully.

Locate the lower 2f string (a transverse string).

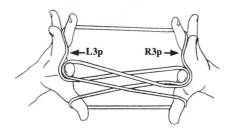

4 picks up lower 2f.

Locate the palmar string that crosses R3 (R3p) and the palmar string that crosses L3 (L3p).

5
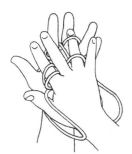 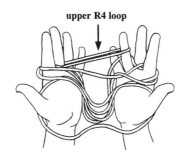 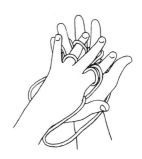

R4 picks up L3p...

...extend partially to create and upper R4 loop...

...L4, over upper R4 loop, picks up R3p...

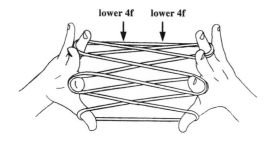

...Extend fully.

Locate the lower 4f string, (a transverse string).

6
 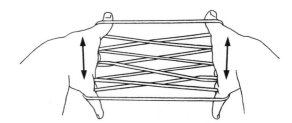

5 picks up lower 4f. To view the basket-shaped *hammock*, point all fingers away from you. You can rock the hammock by pivoting your wrists!

Two Eyes

-collected by James Hornell from the Kru people of Liberia, Africa

Recommended Loop Size: 3 feet

1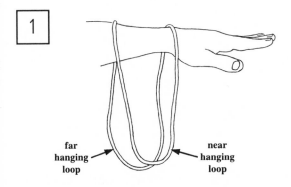

far hanging loop

near hanging loop

Suspend a loop on the L wrist as shown.

Locate the near hanging loop and the far hanging loop.

2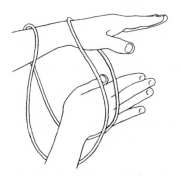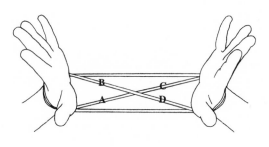

Pass the R hand away from you through the near and far hanging loops...and extend.

Locate the string segments labeled A, B, C, and D.

3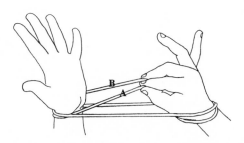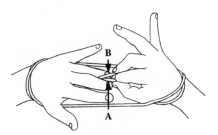

Pinch *segment A* between R1 and R2; pinch *segment B* between R2 and R3, and lift...
...then pinch *segments A* and *B* between L3 and L4...

31

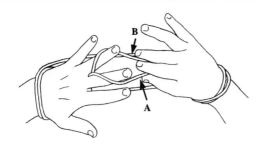

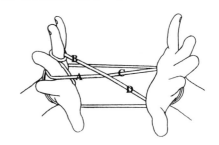

...wrap *segment A* around L3; wrap *segment B* around L4...release R1, R2, R3, and extend. *Again locate string segments A, B, C, and D.*

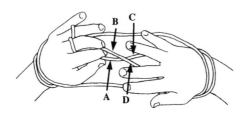

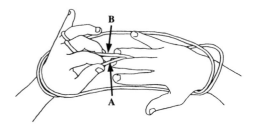

Pinch *segment A* (not *D*!) between L1 and L2; pinch *segment B* (not *C*!) between L2 and L3, and lift...then pinch *segments A* and *B* between R3 and R4...

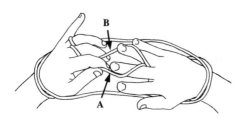

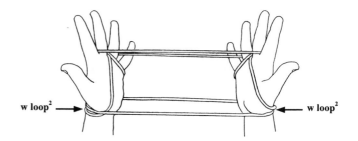

...wrap *segment A* around R3; wrap *segment B* around R4...release L1, L2, L3, and extend. *Locate the double wrist loop (w loop^2).*

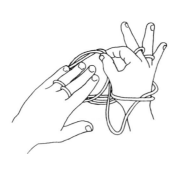

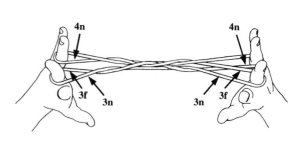

With the help of the R hand lift the double L wrist loop off the L hand and release it. Likewise, lift the double R wrist loop off the R hand and release it (not shown). Extend. *Locate the 3n string, 3f string, and the 4n string.*

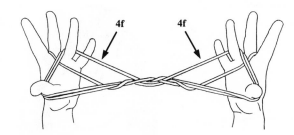

1, over 3n, picks up 3f and 4n.

Locate the 4f string.

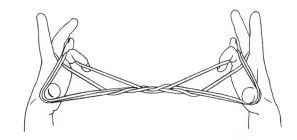

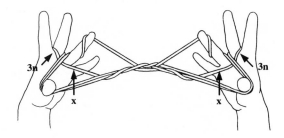

4 hooks up 4f...thus wrapping 4f around the tip of 4.
Locate the string segment marked "x" (a continuation of 3n).

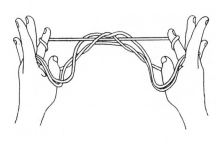

1 hooks down *segment x...*

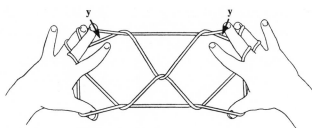

...Extend, palms away from you (the double 1 loop will slip off in the process).

Locate the string segment marked "y."

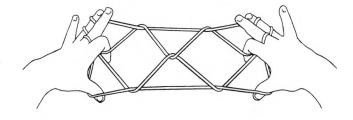

With 2, hook down *segment y.* This improves the symmetry of the design. You have "Two Eyes."

Little Girl with Pigtails

-a traditional Japanese string figure
described by Hiroshi Noguchi, Tokyo

Recommended Loop Size: 3 feet

Traditional Japanese string figures often form a series in which one design is transformed into another. There are three designs in the "Girl" series. In forming the last design, the maker lays the figure on a flat surface and arranges it.

1

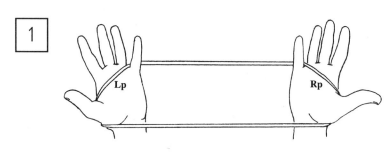

Place loop on 1 and 5.

Locate the L palmar string (Lp), and the R palmar string (Rp).

2

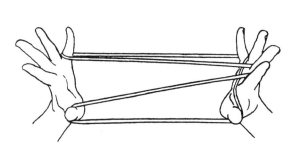

R3 picks up Lp...

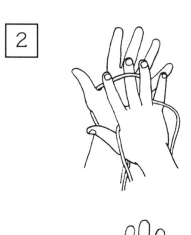

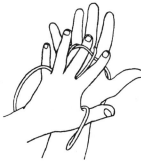

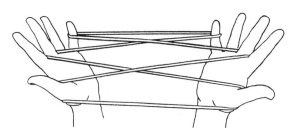

...L3, through R3 loop from above, picks up Rp. The result is known as "Japanese Opening."

34

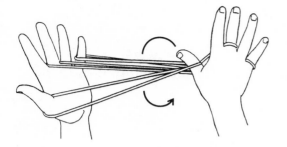

Pass R1 away from you over all the strings...catch the strings on the back of R1...and return R1 to its original position, passing under R1n (which slips off). This move is tricky! You need to pivot the R wrist during the pick up.

Locate the L1 loop.

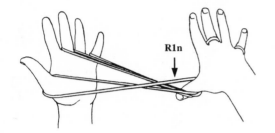

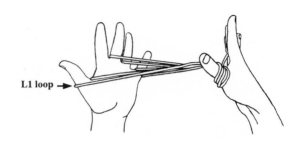

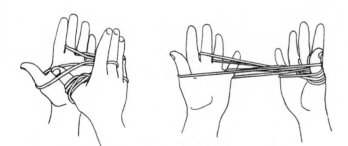

R1, from below, enters the L1 loop and returns to the right.

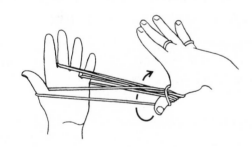

Next, perform Step 3 in reverse (that is, pass R1 towards you, down, away from you under the strings, up, then toward you over the strings).

Locate the upper and lower R1 loop.

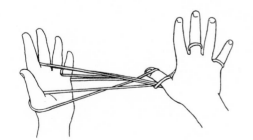

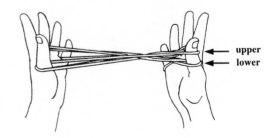

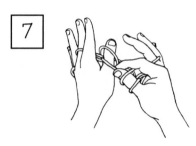

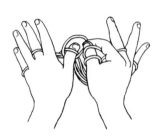

6

L1, from below, enters the upper R1 loop and returns to the left.

7

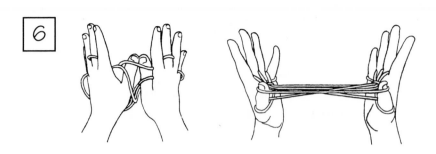

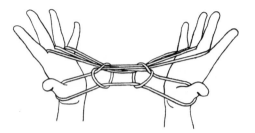

Navaho the L1 loops. Likewise, Navaho the R1 loops (not shown), and extend. *See page 3 for a full description of the Navaho move.*

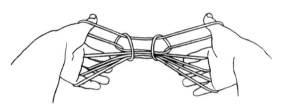

When displayed with fingers pointing away from you, this design represents a "Crab."

8

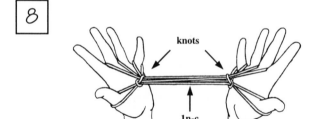

Return hands to the upright position, then separate the hands as far as possible so that the two circular loops near the center collapse and form "knots" around the other strings.

This design represents "Natto" — a traditional Japanese bean food.

Locate the central segment of 1n (1n-c) — the segment between the two knots.

9

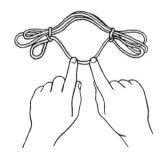

With the fingers pointing upward, lay the figure on a flat surface and pull string 1n-c towards you.

You have the face of a little girl, complete with pigtails!

The Sandsnipe

-collected by Harry and Honor Maude
from the people of Kiribati, Micronesia

Recommended Loop Size: 4 feet

Sandsnipes (sandpipers) are shore birds that feed on fish. In this series of four designs many magical transformations take place as a result of the asymmetric opening. Honor Maude, the world's foremost authority on Oceanic string figures, highly recommends this series.

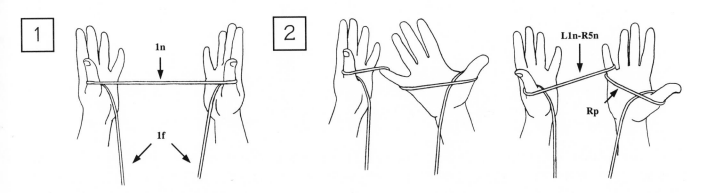

Place loop on 1 so that 1n is short and 1f is long.

Pass R5 toward you *over* 1n, then catch 1n on its back...and return.

Locate the L1n-R5n string and the Rp string.

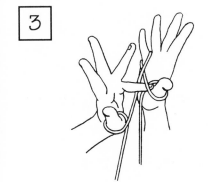

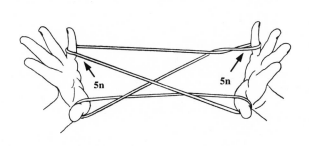

L5, over L1n-R5n, picks up Rp. Extend fully to absorb the hanging 1f string.

Locate the 5n string.

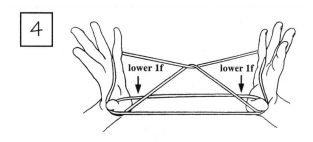

4   1 picks up 5n. *Locate the lower 1f string.*

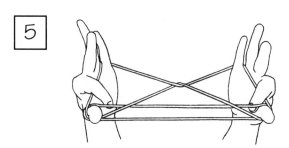

5   With the tip of 2, pick up the 1f string...then press 1 against the side of 2 to prevent the short 1f-2n string from slipping...as you turn the palms away from you to extend the figure.

Step 5 is known as the Caroline Extension.

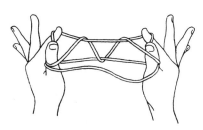

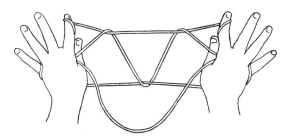

You have "Catching Kingfish," the first design in the series. The long, hanging loop represents the lower bill of the Sandsnipe, which is used to snatch up fish. Technically speaking this is a marvelous figure: the hanging loop remains slack no matter how tightly the strings are drawn!

 6

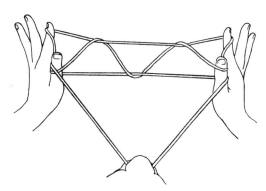

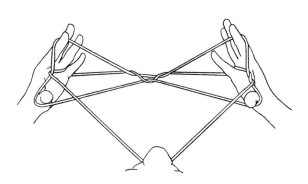

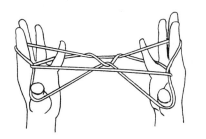

With your mouth grasp the hanging loop...

...lift it over finger 1 on each hand...

...and release it. Extend.

38

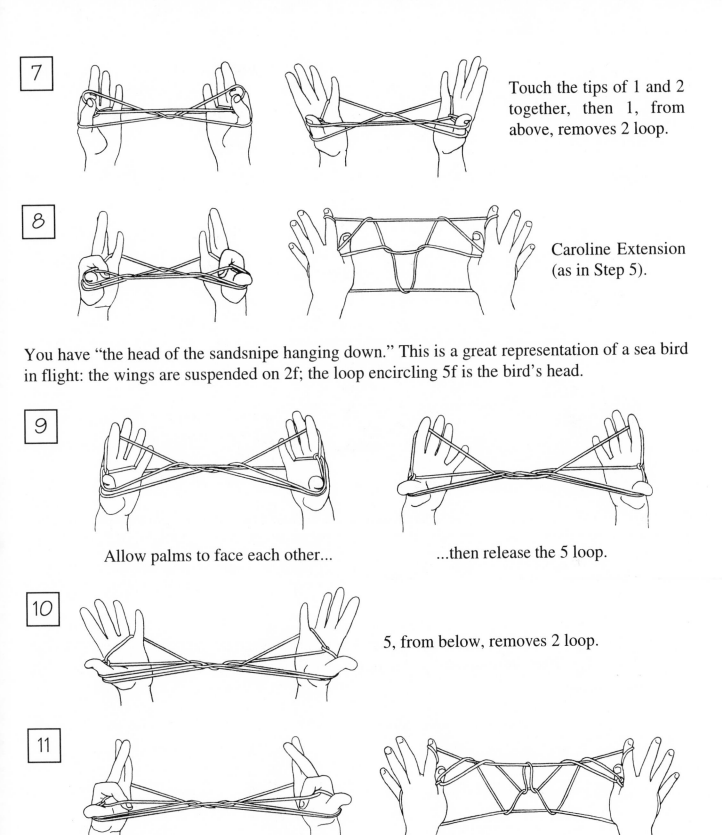

7 Touch the tips of 1 and 2 together, then 1, from above, removes 2 loop.

8 Caroline Extension (as in Step 5).

You have "the head of the sandsnipe hanging down." This is a great representation of a sea bird in flight: the wings are suspended on 2f; the loop encircling 5f is the bird's head.

9 Allow palms to face each other...

...then release the 5 loop.

10 5, from below, removes 2 loop.

11 Caroline Extension. You have "the head of the sandsnipe erect," another splendid representation of a hovering seabird.

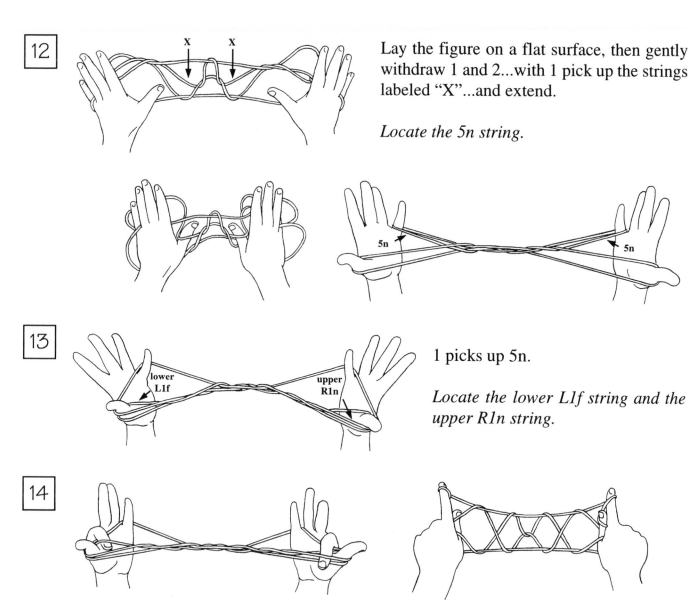

12 Lay the figure on a flat surface, then gently withdraw 1 and 2...with 1 pick up the strings labeled "X"...and extend.

Locate the 5n string.

13 1 picks up 5n.

Locate the lower L1f string and the upper R1n string.

14

L2 picks up lower L1f; R2 picks up upper R1n...Caroline Extension (close 3, 4 and 5 to the palm if you like). Remarkably, a symmetrical four-diamond figure results from this asymmetric maneuver!

15

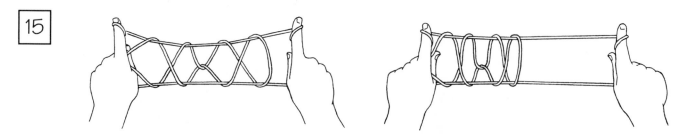

Now for the final surprise — Release the R1 loops...and slowly separate the hands. The diamonds will slide to the left. The islanders call this figure "Flight of the Vanquished," but it could just as easily represent four sandsnipes flying away.

A Toad and a Man

-collected by Julia Averkieva from the
Kwakiutl of Vancouver Island, Canada

Recommended Loop Size: 3 feet

1

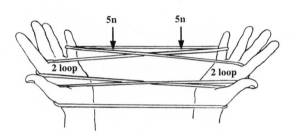

Do Steps 1 and 2 of "A Girl" (page 34), but use finger 2 to pick up the palmar strings. *Locate the 2 loop and the 5n string.*

2

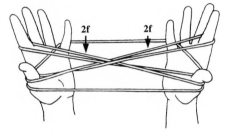

1, under 2 loop, picks up 5n.

Locate the 2f string.

3

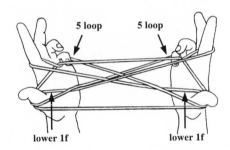

5 hooks down 2f, closing it to the palm (the old 5 loop slips off).

Locate the new 5 loop and the lower 1f string.

4

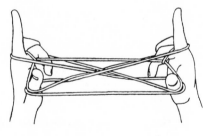

3, "from below*," enters the 5 loop...then passes toward you under the strings and enters the lower 1 loop from above...then hooks up the lower 1f string, drawing it through the 5 loop as it returns.

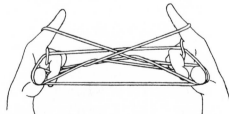
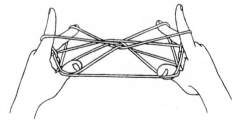

Remember that entering a loop "from below" always means "from the knuckle side" whereas "from above" means "from the fingertip side."

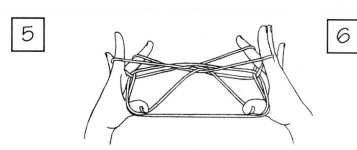

Release 5 loop and extend.

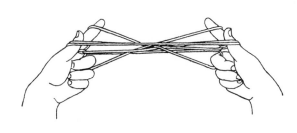

Rotate 3 half a turn away from you and close it to the palm (along with 4 and 5).

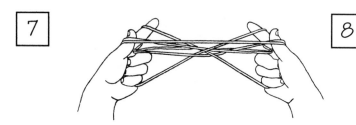

4 and 5, "from below" enter the 3 loop.

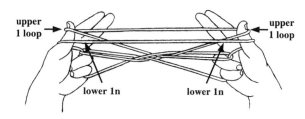

Withdraw 3 from its loop, then release 2 loop and extend. *Locate the upper 1 loop and the lower 1n string.*

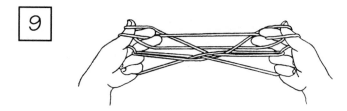

2 and 3, through upper 1 loop from above, grasp lower 1n...then 2 (with the help of 3) hooks up lower 1n, drawing it through the upper 1 loop.

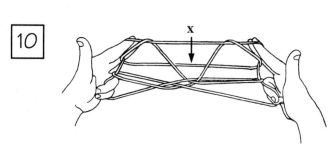

Release 1 loops and extend.

Locate the string segment marked "X."

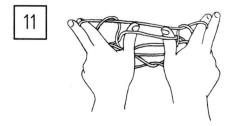

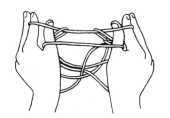

1 picks up segment "X"...then enters the 2 loop from below...

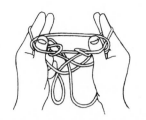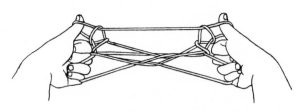

...Navaho the 1 loops (see page 3)...release 2 loop and extend.

At this stage the weaving is complete. In the next step the entire figure is rotated a quarter turn clockwise. Don't panic, it's easier than it looks! Just remember that when entering loops, "from above" and "from below" mean "from the fingertip side" and "from the knuckle side."

 12

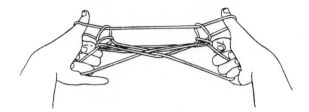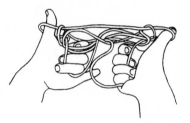

Withdraw L5 from its loop...

L5, "from below," removes the R45 loop...

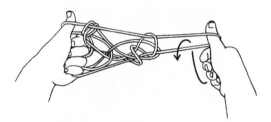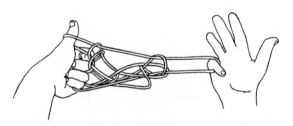

...and returns to the left...

...R5, from above, removes the R1 loop; close R5 to the palm...

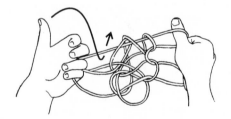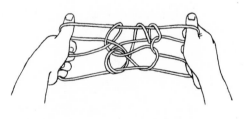

...R1, from below, removes the L1 loop...

...and returns to the right...

...L1, "from above" removes the L4 loop...

...Extend to see "a toad and a man."

In this Native American figure, the zig-zag design on the right represents the legs of a toad; the crooked design on the left represents a man.

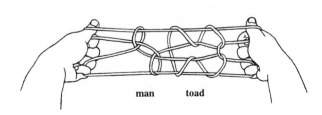

man   toad

43

A Swan

-collected by Diamond Jenness from
the Mackenzie Delta Inuit of Canada

Recommended Loop Size: 3 feet

All sorts of animals inhabit the Arctic regions of Canada, many of which are immortalized in string by the Inuit (Eskimos) who live there. "Swan" is certainly one of their most realistic figures. This interpretation of Jenness's instructions was submitted by Tetsuo Sato of Japan.

| 1 | 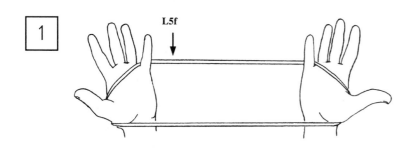 | Place loop on 1 and 5. *Locate the left segment of the 5f string (L5f).* |

| 2 | 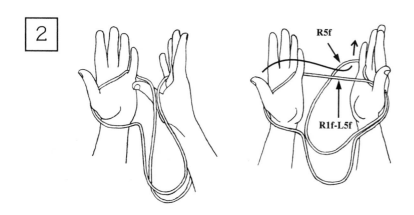 | R1, *over* L5f, picks up L5f... ...Extend partially. *Locate the R1f-L5f string and the R5f string.* |

| 3 | 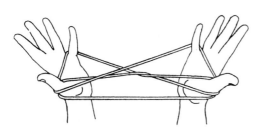 | | 4 | 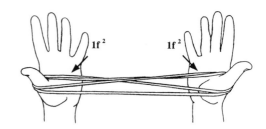 |

L1, over R1f-L5f (but under R5f), picks up R5f. Extend.

Release 5 loop. *Locate the double 1f string.*

44

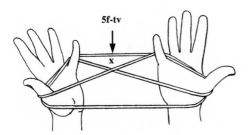

5 picks up 1f^2.

Locate the 5f string which is transverse* (5f-tv).

*A transverse string is a string that runs straight across the figure between two like fingers, in this case R5 and L5.

 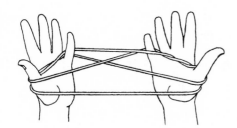 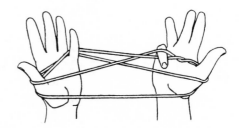

Allow 5f-tv to slip off R5...

...then close R5 to the palm over it...

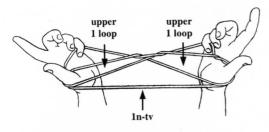

Repeat on L5 and extend.

Note: this move is tricky! In slipping 5f-tv, you need to pass 5 of each hand down through the triangle marked "x" in the Step 5 illustration , then up behind 5f-tv before closing it to the palm.

Locate the 1n-tv string and the upper 1 loop.

 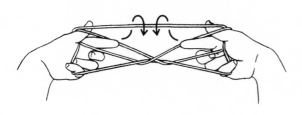

Insert 2, from above, into the upper 1 loop (shown here is the view from below) then curl 2 around 1n-tv...

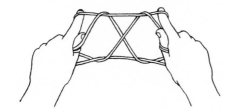

...and return with it through the upper 1 loop by rotating 2 away and up.

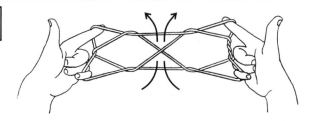

Release 1 loops and extend. You know have a "two-diamond" pattern.

If you made it this far, congratulations! But before proceeding, carefully examine all the string crossings to make sure they match the picture. If they don't, you won't get a swan at the end!

9

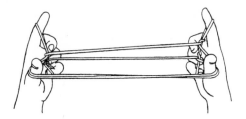

With 1 pick up the two strings that cross in the center, as illustrated above.

10

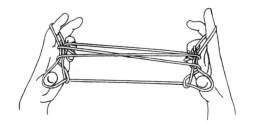

1, from below, enters 2 loop...

Navaho 1 loops (lower double loop over upper single loop).

11

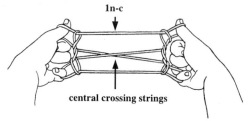

Release 2 loop and extend, 1 pointing upward.

Locate the central segment of the 1n string (1n-c), and the two strings which cross in the center.

12

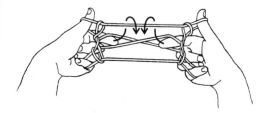

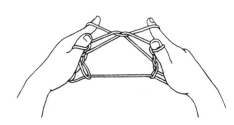

Insert 2, towards you, between the crossing strings, then curl 2 around 1n-c...

...and return with it through the space between the crossing strings.

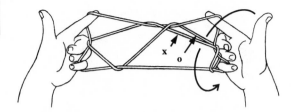

Release 1 loops and extend.

Locate the strings marked "x" and "o.".

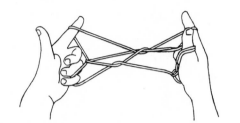

Insert R1, from below, into the R2 loop, then pick up strings "x" and "o" as illustrated above.

This move is rather awkward — fingers usually pass under, not over, strings when picking them up!

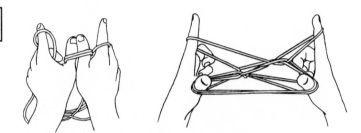

Insert L1, from below, into the double R1 loop...and extend.

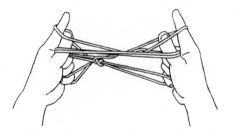

1, from below, enters the 2 loop...

Navaho 1 loops (double lower loop over upper single loop).

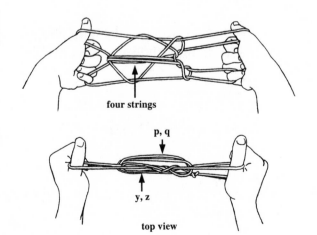

four strings

p, q

y, z

top view

Release 2 loop and extend, 1 pointing upward.

The final two steps are the most difficult. First, locate the four horizontal strings (p, q, y, and z) that cross the center of the figure. If you view the figure from the top, you will see that two of these strings (p, q) pass across the "back" of the figure.

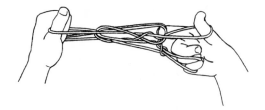

With R2, hook up strings *p* and *q*...

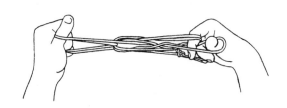

...then insert R2, from above, into the R1 loop.

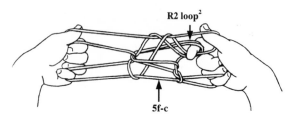

Here is a "front" view. Strings *p* and *q* now form a double R2 loop.

Locate the central segment of the 5f string (5f-c).

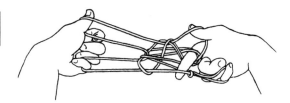

With R2, hook up 5f-c...

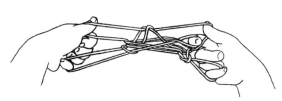

...and draw it through R2 loop^2, which slips off...

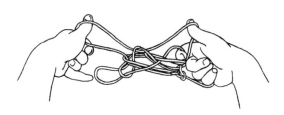

...release the L5 loop...

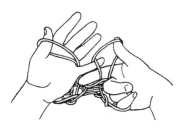

...then L5, through the R1 loop from below, removes the new R2 loop "from above"...

...and returns to the left. Extend and arrange as needed to display the magnificent "Swan."

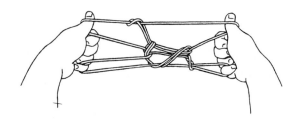

According to the Inuit, Swan asks: To what place are you following me? To the river? I'm afraid! I'm going to fly away! Honk! honk! honk!

If you then release the 5 loop and extend, you get a small circle suspended between two frame strings. This represents the empty lake from which the swan flew.

Sun

-collected by Honor Maude from the
people of Nauru Island, Micronesia
-introduced and illustrated by Joseph
D'Antoni, Queens, New York

Recommended Loop Size: 3 feet

Here is one of my favorite string figures. It is a relatively simple figure to construct. With just a few quick movements a beautiful figure, likened to a sun in some cultures, stretches between your hands. This string figure, and others which look like it except for string crossing details, is made by many different methods. The figure enjoys a worldwide distribution, but it is curiously absent from Eskimo string figures.

Many finished string figures are crisscrossed with string, which an unaccustomed eye might call messy. What I enjoy about this figure is the way the sun is delicately supported by the frame lines. Also, the parallel strands tug at the center, drawing attention to a hollow space conspicuously devoid of all string.

Readers can make the Sun by following step-by-step illustrations. Arrows are used to indicate what needs to be done next.

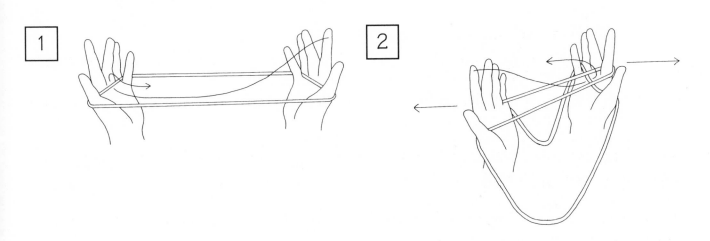

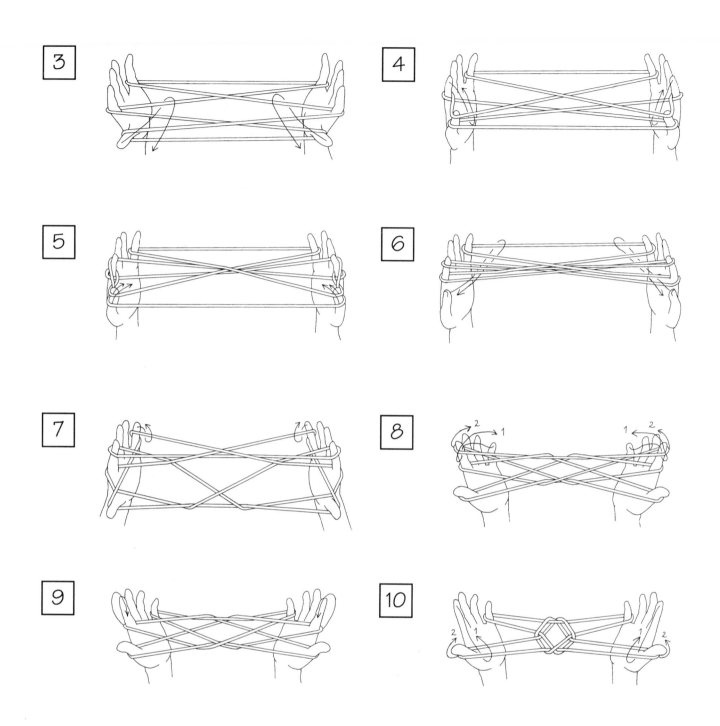

In some parts of the world, the figure shown in illustration 10 is considered complete even though the strings hang limply, and the central part of the figure tends to collapse. Pacific islanders invented a clever way of displaying this and other figures using a technique known as the *Caroline Extension*. Applying this extension accomplishes much. It allows you to have a better hold of the strings, it widens the figure, it removes slack from the strings, and overall, it enhances the way the final figure appears.

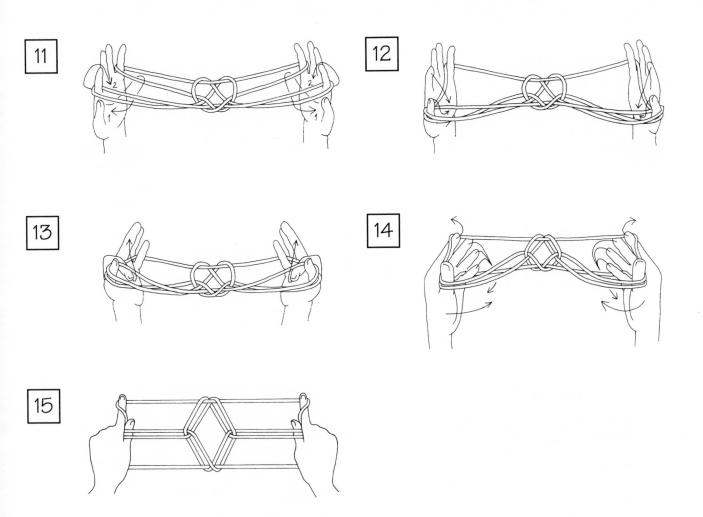

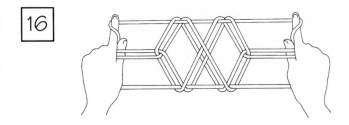

Now that you have seen how the Sun is made, let me challenge you. How can two suns, shown in illustration 16, be made? Hint: With the string on your hands as shown in Step 9, repeat an earlier sequence of movements.

With a long, thin string, I have been able to make five suns. How skillful are you?

Wheelbarrow

-invented by Carey C.K. Smith,
Stratford, New Zealand

Recommended Loop Size: 4 feet

1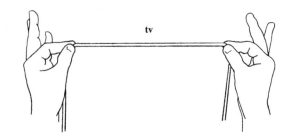

With 1 and 2 grasp a short segment of
the string loop. *Locate the transverse
(tv) string.*

2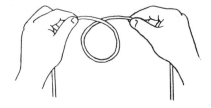

Pass the left portion of the
transverse string in front of
the right portion to form a
small hanging loop.

3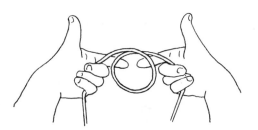

Grasp the side strings with 3, 4, and 5. Release 1, then insert 2, from far side, into the
small hanging loop. Place the loop on 2 by rotating 2 down, away from you, and up.

4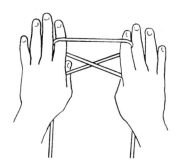

Insert 1, from the near side, into the large hanging loop, releasing 3, 4, and 5. Extend.
In the string figure literature, Steps 1-4 are referred to as the "Navaho opening."

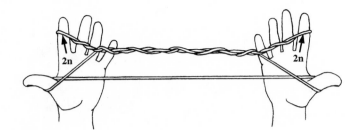

Rotate the 2 loop six full turns toward you.

Locate the 2n string.

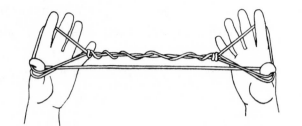

1 picks up 2n.

There are now two loops on each finger 1. The upper loop encircles finger 1 and finger 2.

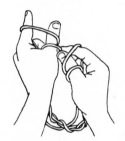  

Navaho the L1 loops (lift the lower loop over the upper loop and release it)...Likewise, Navaho the R1 loops (not shown)...and extend.

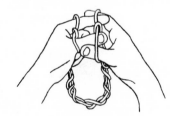

L1, from above (that is, from the fingertip side), removes the R1 loop; L2, from above, removes the R2 loop.

R2, from below (that is, from the knuckle side), removes the upper L1 loop.

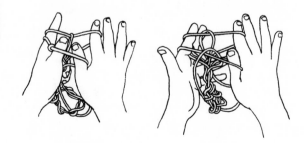

R1, from below, removes the remaining L1 loop.

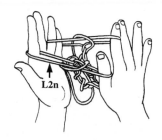

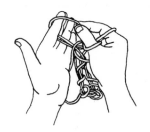

L4 and L5, acting as one finger, remove the upper L2 loop from below. *Locate the L2n string.*

With R1 and R2 grasp L2n; withdraw L2 from its loop, then re-insert it (along with L1) into the same loop, but from the opposite side (that is, toward you).

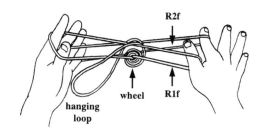

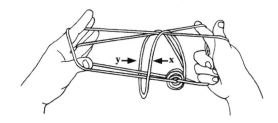

Extend the figure partially until a "wheel" begins to form in the center. A hanging loop will form to the left of the wheel. *Locate the R2f and R1f strings.*

Insert R3, R4, and R5, from above, into the R2 loop, then the R1 loop, closing R2f and R1f to the right palm. *Locate string x and string y.*

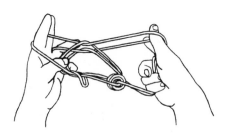

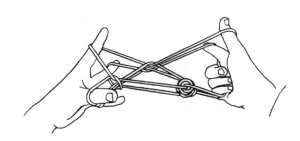

L1 hooks string x to the left and draws it down through the L1-L2 loop; at the same time L5 hooks string y to the left and draws it down through the L4-L5 loop. Extend in three dimensions to complete the wonderfully realistic "Wheelbarrow." Shown below are two additional views.

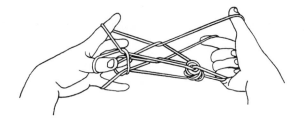

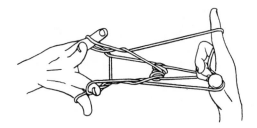

Erupting Volcano

-collected by Raul Martinez-Crovetto
from the Araucano people of
Northern Patagonia, Argentina

Recommended Loop Size: 4 feet

1

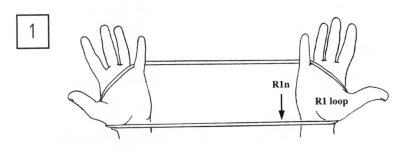

Place loop on 1 and 5.

Locate the R1 loop and R1n string.

2

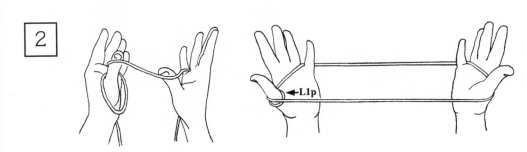

L1, from below, enters R1 loop and picks up R1n. Extend.
Locate the string that crosses the palmar surface of L1 (L1p).

3

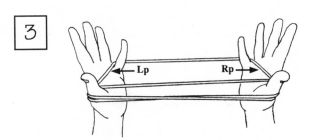

R1 picks up L1p. *Locate the right and left palmar strings (Lp and Rp).*

4

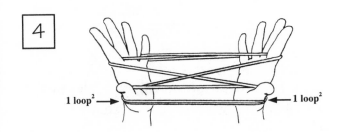

R2 picks up Lp; L2, through R2 loop from above, picks up Rp, as in "Opening A" (see page 5).
Locate the double loop that encircles finger 1.

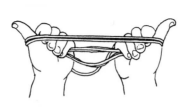 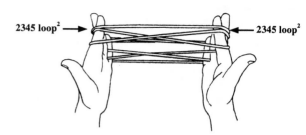

2, 3, 4, and 5, from above, remove the double 1 loop. *Locate the double 2345 loop.*

 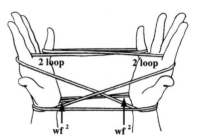

1, from below, enters the double 2345 loop. Allow the double loop to slip down onto the wrists. *Locate the 2 loop and the double far wrist string (wf^2).*

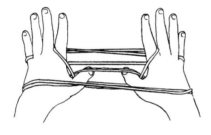 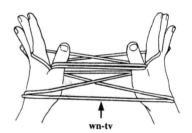

7

1, through 2 loop from above, picks up wf^2 and returns through 2 loop. *Locate the transverse near wrist string (wn-tv).*

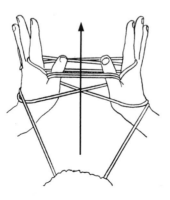 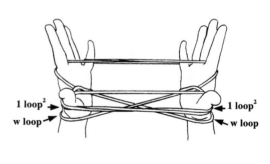

8

With your mouth, grasp the wn-tv string and lift it over all the fingers, releasing it on the far side of the hands (this eliminates one of the wrist loops)...Extend. *Locate the wrist loop and the double 1 loop.*

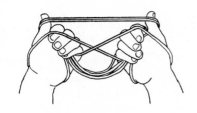 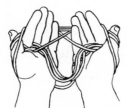 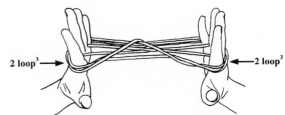

2, 3, 4, and 5, from above, remove the double 1 loop and wrist loop. *You now have a triple loop on each finger 2. Two of these three loops also encircle fingers 3, 4, and 5.*

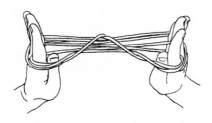 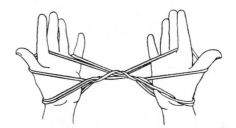

1, from below, enters the triple 2 loop. Allow the double loop that surrounds all five fingers to slip down onto the wrist.

 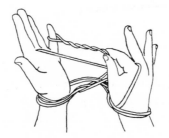 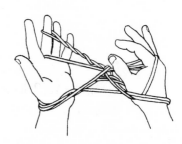

With R1 and R2 grasp both strings of the L5 loop...

...rotate L5 three full turns away from you to twist the loop...

...then lift the loop off L5 and transfer it to L3, releasing R1 and R2...

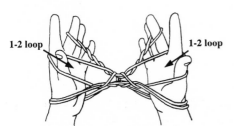

...Repeat on the right hand (not shown)...and extend.

Locate the loop encircling fingers 1 and 2.

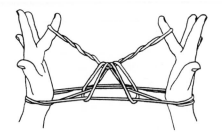

Release the 1-2 loop and extend to produce the three-dimensional "Volcano" (three views are shown here).

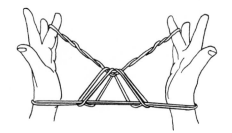

The twisted loops emanating from the cone represent smoke.

This unusual figure has not been observed elsewhere in South America. The fellow who collected it believes that the Araucano people invented or acquired it long ago, during a time when volcanic activity in the region was much greater.

A Dog With Large Ears

-collected by Diamond Jenness
  from the Copper Eskimos, Canada
-introduced and illustrated by
  Joseph D'Antoni, Queens, New York

Recommended Loop Size: 4 feet

Thousands of string figures are known. After showing someone a finished pattern, more often than not, the question "What is it?" will follow. But such is not the case here. The string image of *A Dog With Large Ears* is rather apparent to anyone who has ever seen a dog. As amazingly realistic as this figure already is, there is another feature that makes *A Dog With Large Ears* even more spectacular. As your hands separate, the dog runs along the top and bottom frame lines! Pull the dog back to its starting position and it can run again and again.

Out of the dozens of times I have shown this figure to children and adults, it has never failed to evoke a smile or laughter. In the world of string figures, I cannot think of a more authentic string representation than this one. *A Dog With Large Ears* is by far my most favorite string figure of all.

This is a fairly difficult figure to make, so carefully follow the step-by-step illustrations. For reasons that I will not weary the reader with, I have modified Jenness' original instructions so that my illustrations show the dog running to the left. Of course, some amount of rearrangement will be necessary in order to make the dog stand out best. Also, the kind of string used is a crucial factor in the dog's appearance. An 1/8 inch thick braided nylon cord softens curves and leaves the ears and face round. Since it is often very difficult to describe in words how to manipulate the strings because of unusual finger and hand orientations, I offer not a single word of text. Instead, arrows indicate the next move.

 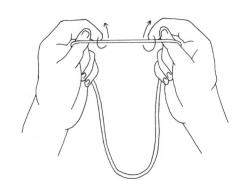

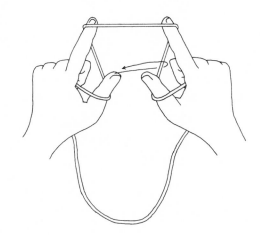

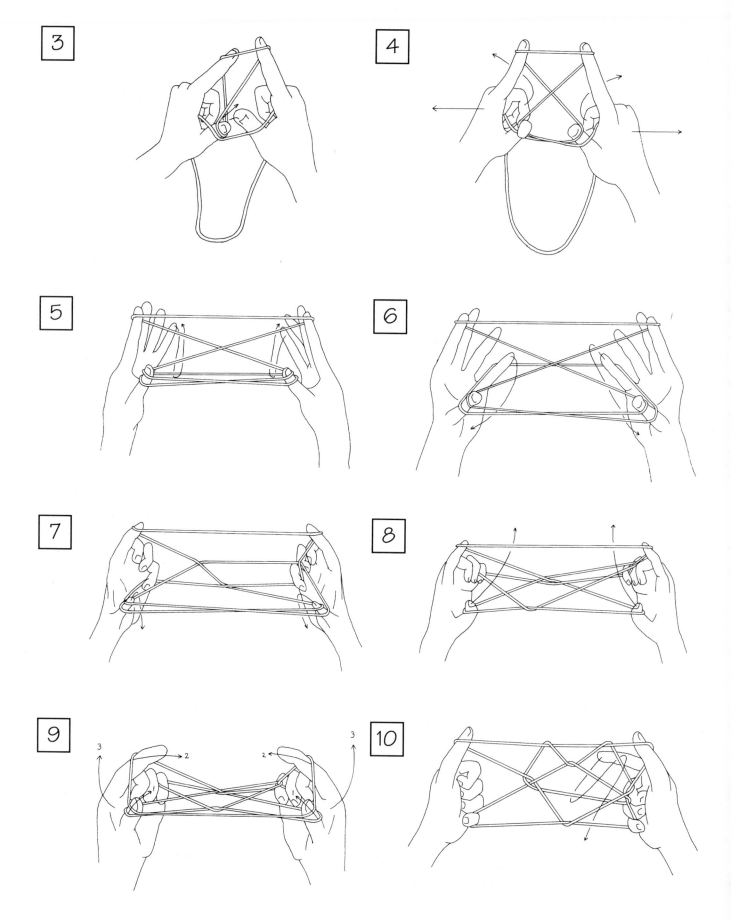

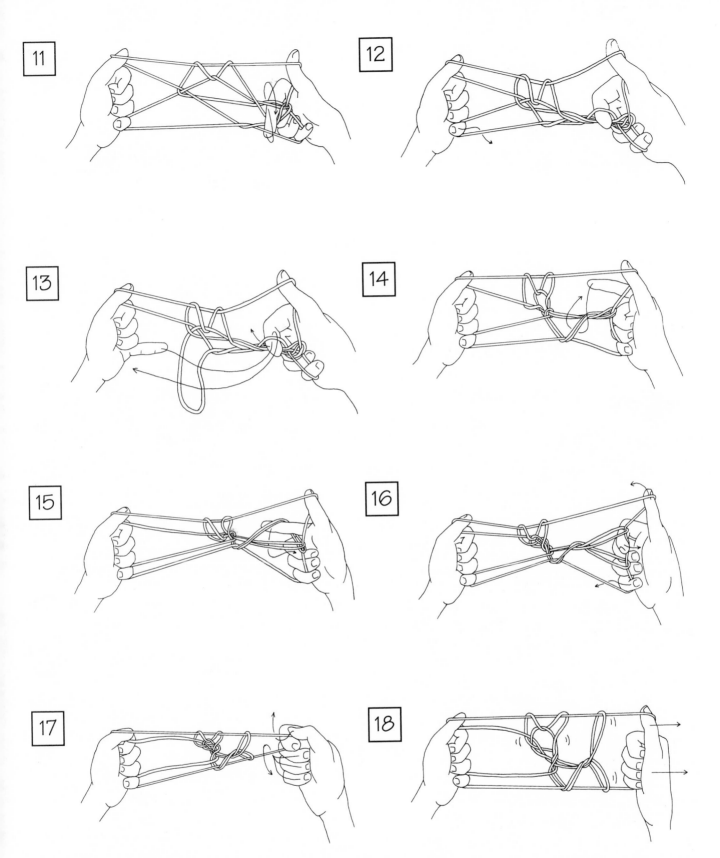

You have "A Dog With Large Ears." To make him run, pull on the string held by the right hand. The dog will slide to the left along the frame strings.

To make the dog run again, reset the strings as shown below...

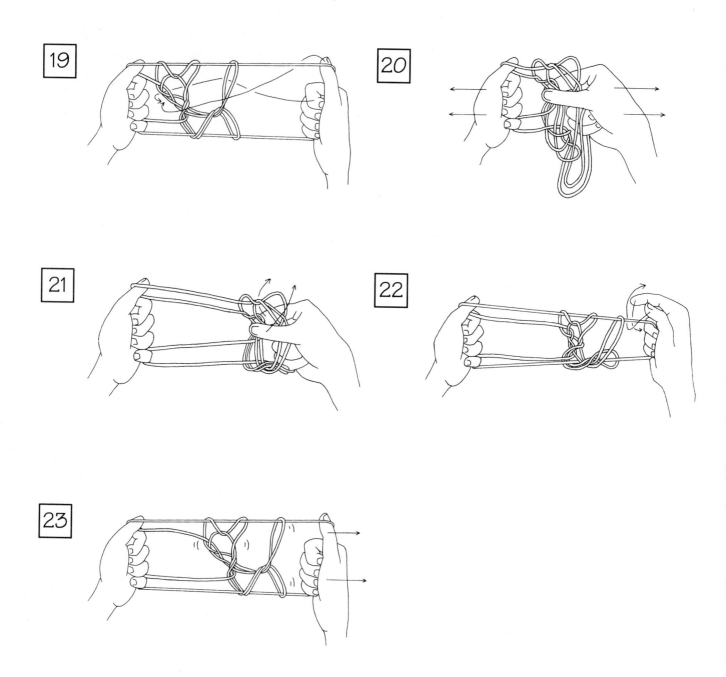

Spectacles for your Nose

-invented by Udo Engelhardt,
Berlin, Germany

Recommended Loop Size: 3 feet

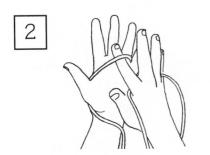

1

Place loop on 1 and 5.
*Locate the L palmar string (Lp),
and the R palmar string (Rp).*

2

R2 picks up L palmar
string...

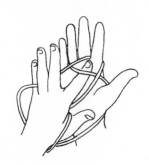
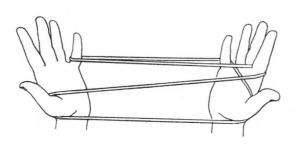

...L2, through R2 loop
from above, picks up R
palmar string. The
result is often called
"Opening A."
Locate the 2 loop.

3

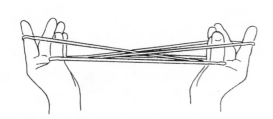
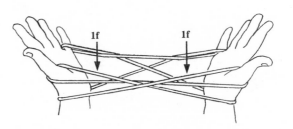

1, 3, 4, and 5, from below, enter the 2 loop. Allow the 2 loop to slip down onto
the wrists. *Locate the 1f string .*

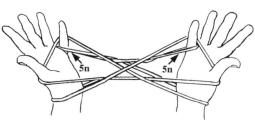

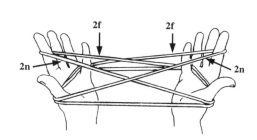

5 picks up 1f. *Locate the 5n string.*

1 picks up 5n. *Locate the wrist loop.*

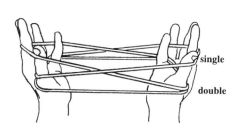

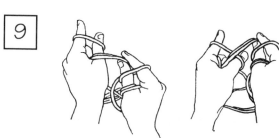

With the help of the opposite hand, lift the wrist loop off the hand and release it. Extend. *Locate the Rp and Lp strings.*

R2 picks up Lp; L2, through R2 loop from above, picks up Lp, as in Opening A. *Locate 2n and 2f.*

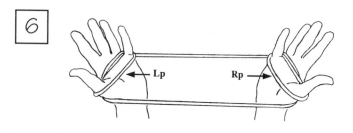

5 picks up 2f; 1 picks up 2n. *You now have a double lower loop and a single upper loop on each 1 and 5.*

Lift the double lower L1 loop over the single upper L1 loop and release it...

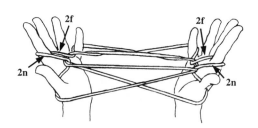

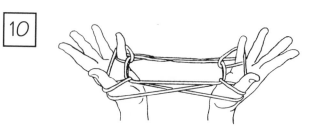

...then repeat on R1, L5, and R5, and extend. *Locate 2n and 2f.*

5 picks up 2f; 1 picks up 2n. Release 2 loop. Extend loosely to form the "lake" (rectangle in the center of the figure).

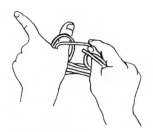 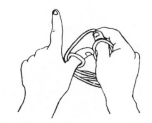 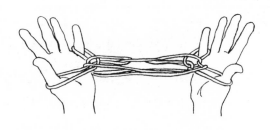

Navaho the L1 loops (lift the lower loop over the upper loop and release it). Repeat on R1, L5 and R5 (not shown), and extend.

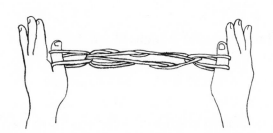

1, from above, removes 5 loop. *You now have a double loop on each 1.*

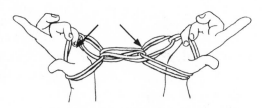

5 hooks down double 1f string, closing it to the palm. *Locate the circular loop near each 5. Each loop is a "lens."*

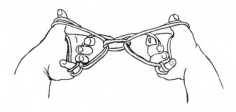

Insert 2, 3, and 4, from above, into the nearest "lens." Point arms away from you to view the figure from below...

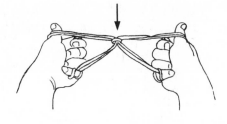

...then enlarge each lens by pulling the side strings toward the palm.
A knot representing the "nose piece" will form in the center.

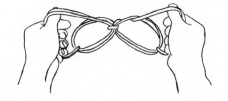

Gently withdraw 2, 3, and 4 to complete the "spectacles."

These spectacles are magic. To wear them, place the outer loops (x) over your ears. Many beautiful things will suddenly appear!

65

The Fox and The Whale

-collected by G. B. Gordon from the
Inuit people of King Island, Alaska
-introduced and illustrated by
Joseph D'Antoni, Queens, New York

Recommended Loop Size: 4 feet

Eskimos are renowned for creating realistic string figures, of which *The Fox and The Whale* is a wonderful example...but such realism has a price. The journey required to produce this figure is long and tortuous, many steps are necessary. In some instances, it is very difficult to describe which string needs to be picked up and exactly how it should be taken because of unusual finger and hand orientations. For this reason, I have abandoned the traditional method of explaining how to make a figure. My goal, here, is to show how to construct *The Fox and The Whale* through illustration. Not a single word of text is offered. Arrows indicate what movements need to be done next.

The figure, collected by G.B. Gordon, originally appeared in print in 1906. My illustrations follow Kathleen Haddon's interpretation of Gordon's instructions. This is a fairly difficult figure to make. Persevere, and success will bring joy. Have fun!

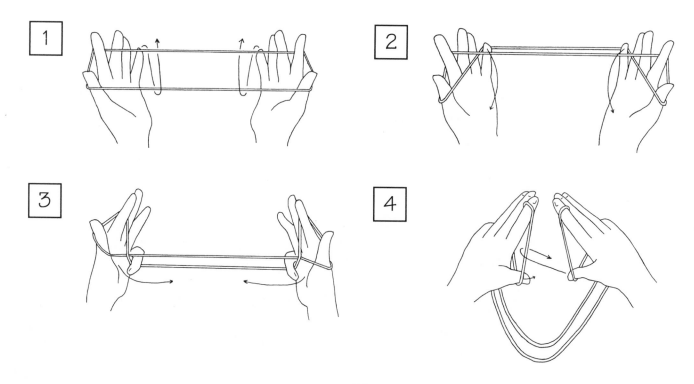

66

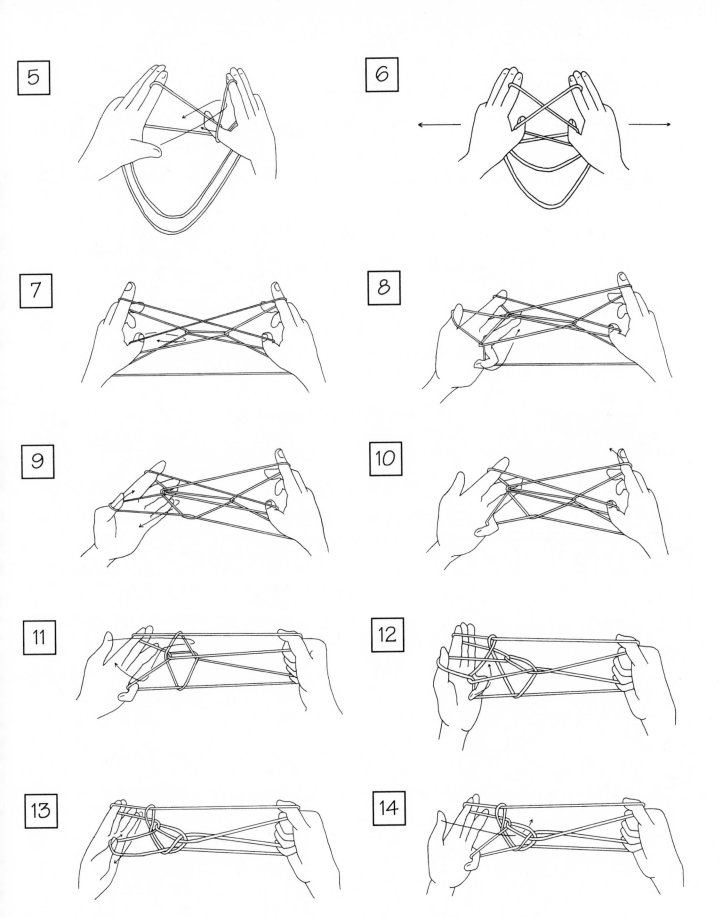

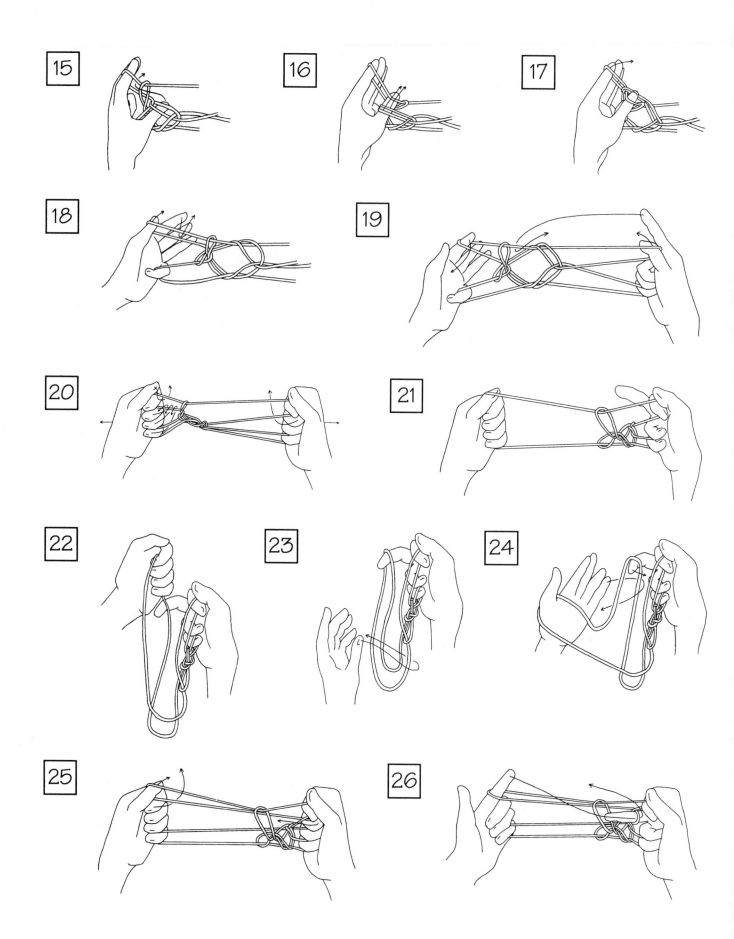

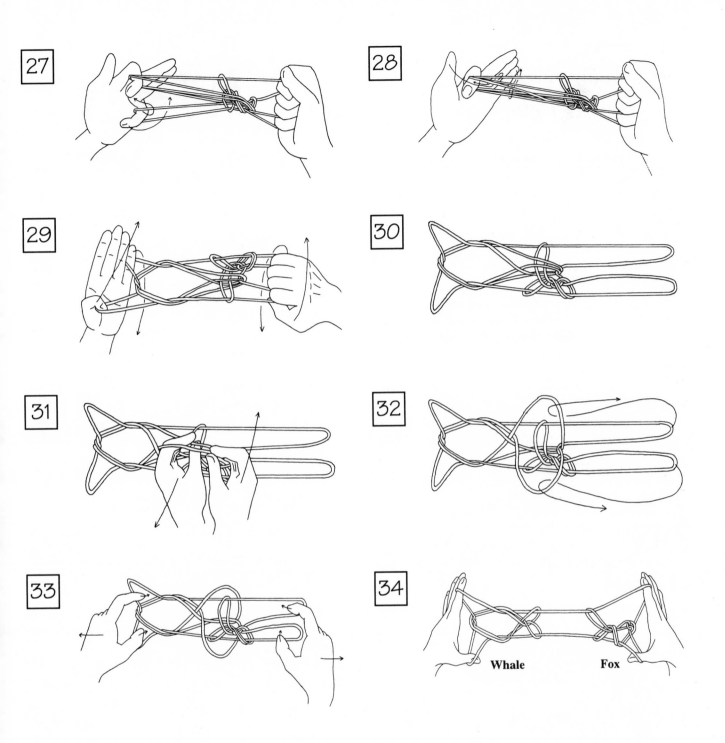

There is a story associated with this figure. A hungry fox comes upon a beached whale and begins to nibble at the carcass. The strings representing fox and whale are snarled together. (Figure 33). Suddenly, someone approaches, and as hands separate, the surprised fox runs from the whale carcass (Figure 34).

Sewing Machine

-collected by H.R. Haefelfinger from
a school girl of Basel, Switzerland

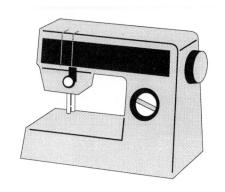

Recommended Loop Size: 3 feet

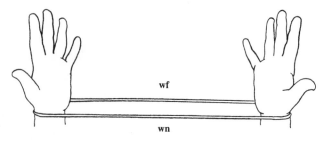

1 Place loop on wrists.

Locate the near wrist string (wn), and the far wrist string (wf).

2

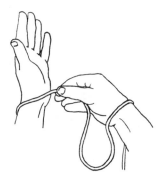

R hand grasps wn...and wraps it once counterclockwise around the L wrist...Release wn and extend.

3

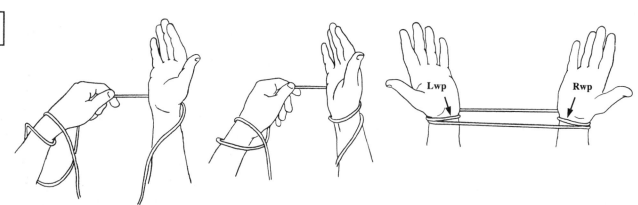

L hand grasps wf...and wraps it once counterclockwise around the R wrist...Release wf and extend. *Locate the left palmar wrist string (Lwp) and the right palmar wrist string (Rwp).*

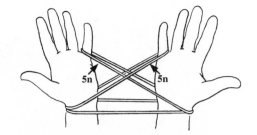

R5 picks up Lwp; L5, through R5 loop from above, picks up Rwp. This move is very much like "Opening A" (see page 5). *Locate the 5n string.*

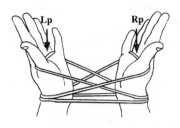

1 picks up 5n. *Locate the left palmar string (Lp) and the right palmar string (Rp).*

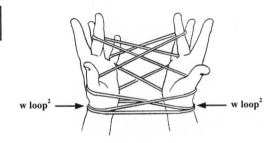

R3 picks up Lp; L3, through R3 loop from above, picks up Rp. Again, this move is much like "Opening A" (see page 5). *Locate the double wrist loop.*

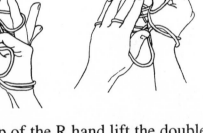

7

With the help of the R hand lift the double L wrist loop off the L hand and release it. Likewise, lift the double R wrist loop off the R hand and release it (not shown).

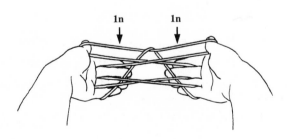

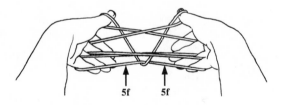

8

Extend, fingers pointing away from you, with the 5f string drawn taut.

This is a splendid action figure! The central V-shaped loop represents the needle of the sewing machine. To make the needle bob up and down, rapidly pivot the forearms so that 1n is drawn taut, then 5f, then 1n, then 5f, and so forth...

Two Islands Joined by a Log

-collected by Walter E. Roth from the Warrau people of Guyana

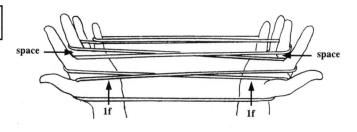

Recommended Loop Size: 4 feet

1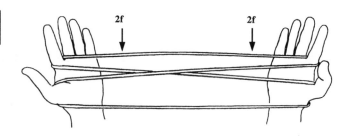

Opening A (see page 5).

2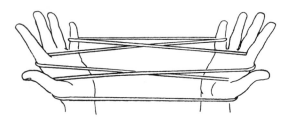

Release 5 loop. *Locate the 2f string.*

3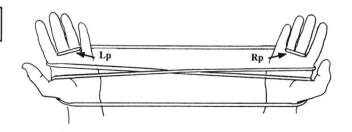

5 picks up 2f, thus creating palmar strings *(Lp and Rp)* crossing the base of 3 and 4.

4

R3 picks up Lp; L3, through R3 loop from above, picks up R palmar string. *Locate the 1f string, and the space between the 2f and 3n.*

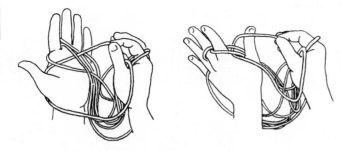

R1 and R2, from above, enter the space between L2f and L3n; Pass the two fingers under the L2 loop, grasp the L1f string, and draw it out...

...Bring the string towards you, over the L2 loop, and place it on L1 so that the string becomes an upper L1n string...

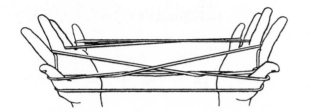

...Repeat on the R hand and extend.

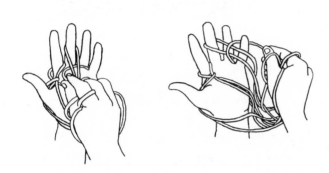

Again R1 and R2, from above, enter the space between L2f and L3n; Pass the two fingers under the L3 loop, grasp the L5n string, and draw it out...

...Pass the string away from you, over the L3 loop, and place it on L5 so that the string becomes an upper L5f string...

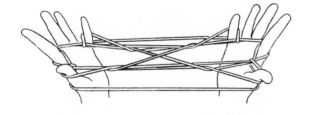

...Repeat on the R hand and extend.

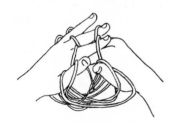 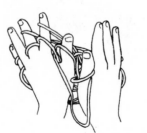 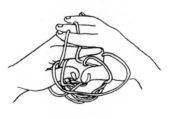

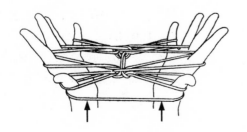

Simultaneously exchange the 2 loops and the 3 loops, inserting the fingers from above, passing R loops through L loops (see page 3). *Locate the lower 1 loop (the loop whose near string is transverse).*

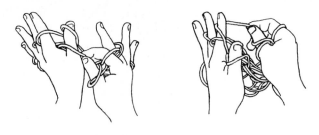

With R1 and R2 grasp the lower L1n string...lift the lower L1 loop over the upper L1 loop and place it on L2 so that the former L1n string becomes an upper L2f string...

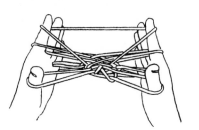

...Repeat on the R hand and extend.

Similarly, locate the lower 5 loop (the loop whose far string is transverse).

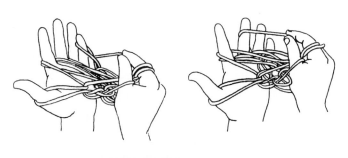

With R1 and R2 grasp the lower L5f string...lift the lower L5 loop over the upper L5 loop and place it on L3 so that the former L5f string becomes an upper L3n string...

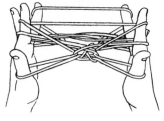

...Repeat on the R hand and extend.

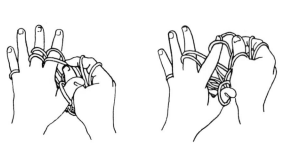

Navaho the L2 loops...Navaho the L3, the R2, and the R3 loops (not shown)...and extend in three dimensions (keep the 2 and 3 loops near the fingertips). You have "Two Islands joined by a Log." View the figure from above to see the log.

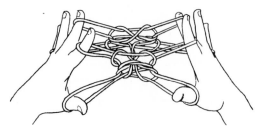

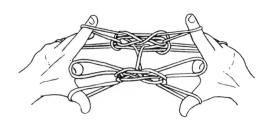

Andromeda Galaxy

-invented by Felix Paturi,
Rodenbach, Germany

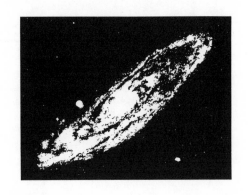

Recommended Loop Size: 5 feet

1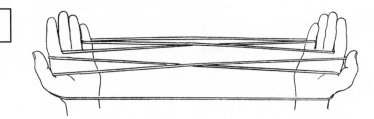

Opening A (see page 5).

2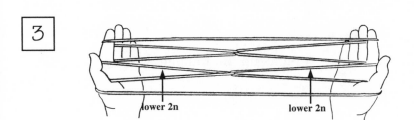

Exchange 2 loops, inserting 2 from above, passing R loop through L loop (see page 3).

3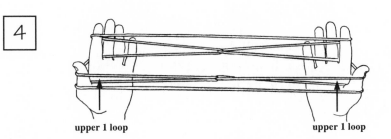

lower 2n   lower 2n

2, from above, removes 5 loop.
Locate the lower 2n string.

4

upper 1 loop   upper 1 loop

1 picks up lower 2n.
Locate the upper 1 loop.

5

Exchange upper 1 loops, inserting 1 from below, passing L loop through R loop...

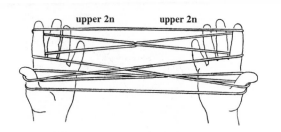 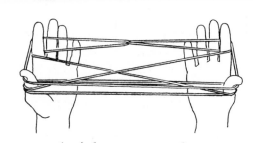

 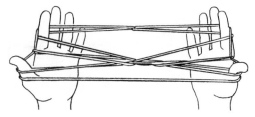

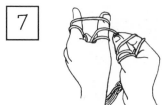

...and extend. *Locate the upper 2n string.*

1 picks up upper 2n.

Navaho middle L1 loop over upper L1 loop...Repeat on R1 (not shown), and extend.

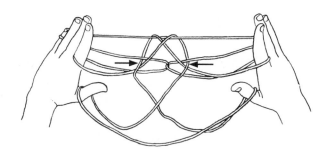

Release upper 2 loop; 5, from above, removes upper 1 loop; extend loosely. *Locate the string segments caught between 2n and 5n.*

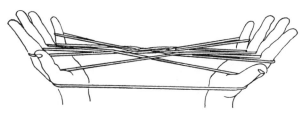

4 picks up the indicated string segments.

3, from above, removes 2 loop.
2 from above, removes 1 loop.
Locate the 3n string.

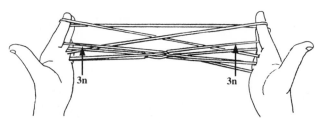

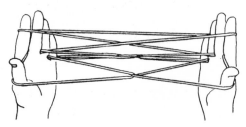 

1, under 2 loop, picks up 3n.

Exchange 1 loops, inserting 1 from below, passing R loop through L loop.

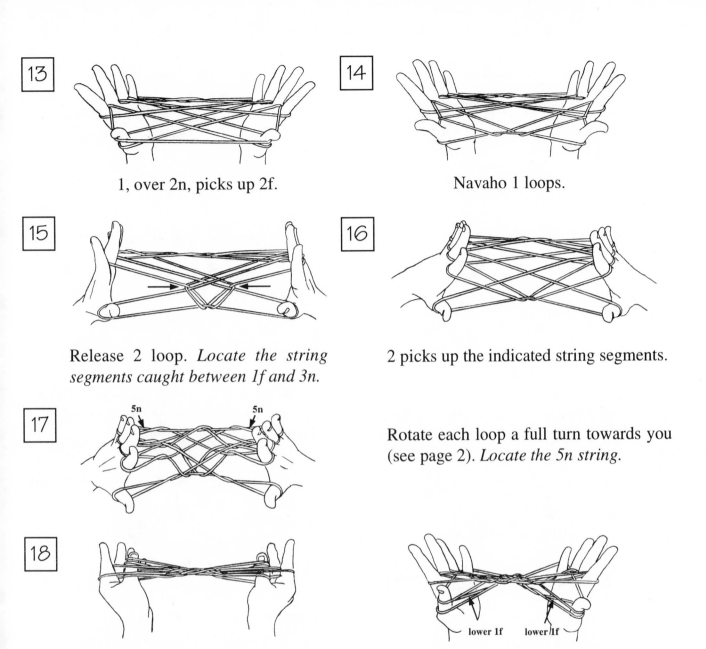

13 1, over 2n, picks up 2f.

14 Navaho 1 loops.

15 Release 2 loop. *Locate the string segments caught between 1f and 3n.*

16 2 picks up the indicated string segments.

Rotate each loop a full turn towards you (see page 2). *Locate the 5n string.*

17

18 Pass 1, from below, through 2 loop, then 3 loop, then 4 loop, and pick up 5n...
Return with 5n through 4, 3, and 2 loop. *Locate lower 1f.*

lower 1f   lower 1f

19

lower 5f

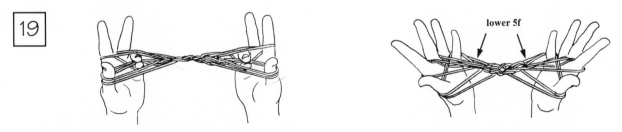

Pass 4 and 5, from above, through 4 loop, then 3 loop, then 2 loop, then upper 1 loop, and pinch lower 1f between them...Return through upper 1 loop, 2, 3, and 4 loop. The former lower 1f string becomes an upper 5 loop. *Locate the lower 5f string, which is transverse.*

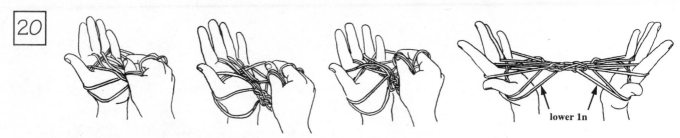

20

With R1 and R2 reach through upper L5 loop from above and grasp lower L5f...Draw it up through upper L5 loop and release both loops from L5...Replace the held loop on L5... Repeat on R hand (not shown) and extend. *Locate the lower 1n string, which is transverse.*

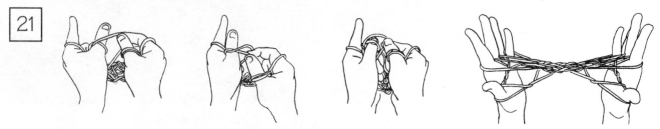

21

With R1 and R2 grasp the lower L1n string and place it above the upper L1 loop...Release R1 and R2, then grasp the new lower L1 loop...Lift it over the new upper L1 loop and off of L1 (i.e. Navaho)...Repeat on R hand (not shown), and extend.

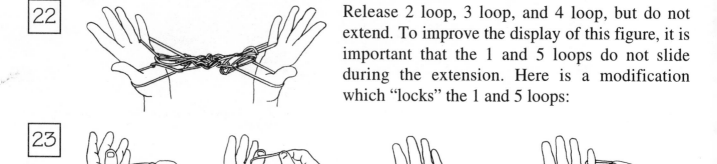

22

Release 2 loop, 3 loop, and 4 loop, but do not extend. To improve the display of this figure, it is important that the 1 and 5 loops do not slide during the extension. Here is a modification which "locks" the 1 and 5 loops:

23

Grasp L1n with R1 and R2...and wrap it once around L1...Likewise, grasp L5f...and wrap it once around L5. Repeat on R1 and R5 (not shown).

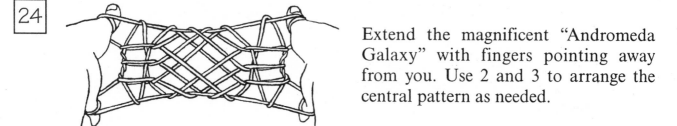

24

Extend the magnificent "Andromeda Galaxy" with fingers pointing away from you. Use 2 and 3 to arrange the central pattern as needed.